OUR MAN ON THE HILL

A British Diplomat Remembers

OUR MAN ON THE HILL

A British Diplomat Remembers

William Mortimer Drower

IGS PRESS
INSTITUTE OF GOVERNMENTAL STUDIES
UNIVERSITY OF CALIFORNIA BERKELEY
1993

©1993 by the Regents of the University of California. All rights reserved.
Printed in the United States of America.

Library of Congress Cataloging-In-Publication Data

Drower, William Mortimer,
    Our man on the Hill : a British diplomat remembers / William
Mortimer Drower.
      p. cm.
      Includes bibliographical references.
      ISBN 0-87772-341-9
      1.Drower, William Mortimer. 2. Great Britain—Foreign relations—United States. 3. United States—Foreign relations—Great Britain. 4. United States—Foreign relations—1963-1969. 5. United States-Foreign relations—1969-1974. 6. Great Britain—Foreign relations—1945- 7. Diplomats—Great Britain—Biography. 8. Diplomats—United States—Biography. I. Title.

DA591.D76A3 1993
327.2'092—dc20
                                                                                                      93-29492
                                                                                                                 CIP

CONTENTS

Foreword	ix
Chapter One Origins	1
Chapter Two School Notes	17
Chapter Three "One People, One Blood"	25
Chapter Four Meeting the Japanese	39
Chapter Five Another Kind of Japan	45
Chapter Six "You Ought To Be Dead"	63
Chapter Seven Liberation-Sudden and Sweet	81
Chapter Eight Back to the East	87
Chapter Nine Egypt After Farouk	103
Chapter Ten Swiss Role	111
Chapter Eleven A Capitol Fellow	121
Chapter Twelve Home To Roost	141

William Mortimer Drower

FOREWORD

In his excellent memoir of his time in Washington, the redoubtable Alan Gotlieb, Ambassador from Canada from 1981 to 1989, describes how difficult it was to learn about the enormous importance of the United States Congress in the American scheme of things. "Like most foreigners," he writes, "I completely failed to understand the U.S. political system."[1]

"The idea of a Canadian diplomat lobbying the Congress just did not seem right. . . . Indeed, it remained the standard practice for many years, until the mid-1970's, for the staff of the Embassy to refrain from this type of activity, and, for most officers of the Embassy, Capitol Hill was off limits."[2]

Needless to say, the bulk of Gotlieb's book is about lobbying Congress. By the 1980's, foreigners with a need to know had begun to understand the myriad special features of American politics, of which Capitol Hill and its extraordinarily independent, highly transformative, bicameral legislature is without a doubt the most significant.

Two decades before, from 1964 to 1974, the British Embassy in Washington had already taken Ambassador Gotlieb's point, and established a special Capitol Hill beat, to which the author of this memoir, Bill Drower, was assigned. Mr. Drower modestly cedes priority in the job to the young Isaiah Berlin, whose wartime despatches from Washington showed a superb grasp of American national

---

[1] Alan Gotlieb, *I'll Be With You in a Minute, Mr. Ambassador* (Toronto: University of Toronto Press, 1991), p. 17.

[2] Gotlieb, p. 22.

Foreword

politics. In those years there was no Beltway to be inside, but I. Berlin, as he signed himself, got around what was then a much smaller and less complicated Washington quite successfully.[3]

Even so, in the far larger and more complicated Washington world of the 1960's, Bill Drower looked a lot like a pioneer to the community of American professional Congress-watchers with whom he occasionally crossed paths in the pursuit of his work. Picture if you will a very tall, cultivated, curious, twinkling man, fully in command of the formidably elaborate courtesies of his diplomat's trade, vastly well-informed about the local American politics that impinged upon the flock of Senators and Representatives whose activities he watched, and utterly delighted with the whole spectacle. Bill Drower grasped nuances about America and made friends among Americans with a virtuosity that must have been a great professional asset. It also made his company delightful and rewarding. And so it has remained in the two decades of his "retirement" as he has turned his attention to British local government and to the cultivation of his garden in the West Country of England.

Mr. Douglas Hurd, speaking as Britain's Foreign Secretary, sometimes remarks that in the modern world in which the United Kingdom, shorn of its Empire, occupies a diminished economic position, it is still possible for Britain to "punch above its weight" in world affairs by virtue of the accumulated skills of its well educated and

---

[3]See *Washington Despatches 1941-1945: Weekly Reports From the British Embassy*, edited by H. G. Nicholas (Chicago: University of Chicago Press, 1981).

William Mortimer Drower

experienced corps of diplomats. The attentive reader of this memoir will see a sharp illustration of Mr. Hurd's point. Queen Elizabeth sent no ordinary person to Capitol Hill when the singular responsibility of seeing the broad sweep of American politics from that superb vantage point was confided to Bill Drower. And we are fortunate to have a sketch of Bill's eventful life from the best possible source.

— Nelson W. Polsby
University of California,
Berkeley, California
July, 1993

CHAPTER ONE

ORIGINS

"capital fellow," commented my grandfather on an engineering acquaintance as he supped his breakfast porridge, taken with salt rather than sugar, standing before the dining-room coal fire. "But he's too taken up with this cracked 'technology' talk coming from that scallywag Henry Ford. Depend upon it, we'll soon hear no more of that. Too old at forty, Ford puts about, what disgraceful claptrap! I hope we'll not see the likes of him here." And soon he was putting on his boots, spats, greatcoat and bowler hat to set off to our London suburban railway-station to take his place, armed with a copy of the London *Times*, in a smoke-begrimed compartment for the twenty minute journey to Victoria Station. Thence he was wont to walk the ten minutes to the big Edwardian block housing his office and to disdain mechanical aid, until very old, up the four stair flights to the frosted glass door legend: "Drower and Brighton. Quantity surveyors, 28, Victoria Street." As likely as not he would be greeted by Pinner, the clerk, who would help him off with his coat. His partner usually rolled up a bit

later, an unctuous man, with a flabby handshake. To me he recalled a character out of Dickens. But he was said to enjoy "many useful contacts" in my trusting grandfather's opinion, which may well have been true. Too true perhaps, since on Mr. B's death it was discovered that he had for years maintained a woman, not his wife, with several children, presumably at the cost of the firm.

My grandparents were born and brought up in the West of England, halfway through the 19th century days which saw the peak of the Industrial Revolution, the first steps in public education, the widening of the franchise, something like a journalistic and literary explosion, and the strong expansion in numbers and political power of the British middle class. Enormous world events were also taking place: the Great Cholera Epidemic, the Indian Mutiny, the American War between the States, the consolidation of a dynamic German nationality. In the South of England, from which so many emigrants bound for the Southern States had set out, there was not much sympathy with the Federalists of the North. The year my father's father first saw the light was 1853, a few months before British and French troops launched a bungled and futile campaign against the Russian Empire. John Edmund Drower (J.E.D.) was born in the compact little farming community of Colyton, a few miles from the cathedral city of Exeter. With its ornately towered 14th century church and magnificent tombs, Colyton has little altered since the 18th century, save for recent commuter bungalows on the outskirts. The Drowers possess a rare name, perhaps a corruption of the Flemish, since it seems they came over to Britain in the 13th or early 14th century as weavers.

(One of the reasons given for the English peasant revolts of the 14th century was resentment at the alleged taking of jobs by such immigrants from the continent of Europe.) To London, then to the Home Counties close by and to the West Country the family moved over the years. By 1580 the Drowers had settled as agricultural workers — "husbandmen"— in West Coker, a village of a round one thousand souls then as now where the author lives, set in rolling agricultural land halfway between Salisbury and Exeter.

Here Ursula Drower is on record as having witnessed the bequeathal of a leather jerkin to another villager, her husband having presumably preceded her to the grave. In 1601 one Richard Drower was arraigned for non-payment of a five pound debt, the magistrates deeming that he "should be taken." He was not. In those days a distance of twenty five miles as the crow flies was then quite enough for a man and his family to feel safe, since the inhabitants of nearby villages were often looked on as "foreigners." Thus Richard's sudden move over to Colyton was a prudent means of escape from the arm of mediaeval law. In fact John Jeans, the aggrieved creditor, was asking for the payment of a considerable sum.

After initially lying low for a time, the Drowers appear to have established themselves as labourers and simple artisans. Late in the 17th century Robert, possibly the great grandson of the Coker debtor, became friendly with Colyton's parson, a vigorous opponent of King James II's increasingly pro-Catholic policies. One historian has described Colyton as then being "the most rebellious place in Devon." So when the illegitimate son of King Charles

Origins

II, the shallow but good-looking Duke of Monmouth, landed on the South Coast a few miles away, hoping to topple the king, both young Robert and his brother Zachary joined the rebel banner. In the event Monmouth's untrained and miserably armed forces were easily cut to pieces by the King's army on the misty Somerset marshes. Robert was captured and soon found himself before Judge Jefferies whose commission was to crush all resistance. Lashed by the foul tongue of that able but over-assiduous royal servant, Robert was among the first to be sentenced to death; but later, since he was only sixteen years old and evidently influenced by the anti-royalist parson of Colyton, his sentence was eventually commuted to transportation to Jamaica. For many others in the assizes round the West Country hanging, disembowelling and the seething cauldron were the penalty. Zachary was luckier; he was allowed to go home but subsequently heavily fined by the government. Royalist troops, searching for fugitive rebels, had noticed a tell-tale white shirttail protruding from a waterwheel bucket.

Memories of the revolt and of its savage suppression died hard in the West. It may well have helped the rapid success of the Methodist movement in that part of Britain a century later. Methodism thrived on anti-Establishment resentment, later to be taken up into the liberal-socialist reform coalition. And was it not often said in Victorian times that the Church of England was the Tory party at prayer? Many were the gruesome tales of the 1685 disaster of Monmouth's botched attempt on the throne which were repeated in the fields or in the rush-lit cottages; stories of the Duke's cowardice when told of his sentence of execution; of the leading part played by the Bishop of Bristol from his coach on the battlefield and of the ferocity of revengeful King James, so soon to be chased out of the country and supplanted by a Dutch prince. Over much of the next century and into the Eighteen Fifties, the Drowers in Colyton, split between Dissenters and Anglicans, hardly seem to have taken much part in farm life, rather to have made a fair living as artisans. Several Benjamin Drowers are recorded as "carriers" of goods. My great-grandfather John was remembered by some as the "finest breeches-maker in the West." It seems that he also made shoes for the townspeople, whereas his brother Edmund acted as an insurance agent beside running the village school. One or two old folk twenty years ago still remembered "Ned's school." More lamentably one William Drower is remembered as having become a missionary in Africa in the early part of the 19th century but as having been "eaten of lions."

To return to my grandfather: after village dame's school he seems to have found some private tutoring and took one of the first Oxford Local Examinations in Exeter at the age of fourteen years. Then to nearby Axminster, a market town where relatives lived. It had been from Axminster that a niece of another William Drower, Nancy Dawson, had set out in about 1750 on an ambitious and colourful career as a dancer at Covent Garden and Drury Lane, London's main theatres. She soon became celebrated, and indeed notorious, by dancing a hornpipe in John Gay's satirical "Beggar's Opera." A ballad entitled "Nancy Dawson" was set to the children's rhyme she danced to — "Here we go round the mulberry bush." "Set up" as mistress by a nobleman, she regularly delighted and enraged the Devon townspeople by returning by coach to visit her friends and flaunt her finery. One Mrs. Burch declared she remembered Nancy dancing a minuet at the Dolphin Inn with her petticoats trimmed with silver lace. When she died pretty, young, "heartless, mercenary and immoral," scurrilous verses were anonymously added to her tomb. There is a portrait of Nancy in the Garrick Club in London, traditionally the haunt of actors and wits.

    J.E.D. would have heard the century old scandal, and probably chuckled. He soon set off to the metropolis, though not before having courted the young Devon woman who was to become his wife, Bessie Florence, my grandmother, who to the end of her days said "grass" in the quick West Country way, rather than "grarce," the snob mode of speech. J.E.D. got himself apprenticed to a surveyor and within a few years was a partner in a quantity surveying firm quite close to the British Museum. By the early Eighteen Nineties he had become well-established in his profession and had broken through enough of the rigid Victorian class barriers to be elected a member of the Savile Club, a literary circle whose numbers included Robert Louis Stevenson and Henry James. J.E.D was a keen amateur astronomer. He kept a telescope in a shed in the garden to which on certain occasions he would retire. On two occasions he took me with him to meetings of the Royal Astronomical Society, and I was presented to several astronomers of high distinction, in particular the doyen of the club, Sir James Jeans, who was majestically affable. In old age my grandfather became almost totally blind; I suppose this to have been the result of observing the sun unprotected from its rays save by smoked glass, which, when gamma radiation was unknown, was thought quite adequate.

During the First World War J.E.D. worked at the War Office in Whitehall and occupied a senior post dealing with supplies and equipment contracts, one where a less honest person might plentifully have lined his pockets. His relations with labour union representatives were always correct and to some he was "old bloody politely." Returning after the war to private practice, he exerted himself to improve the status of surveyors, who until then had often been looked upon as the poor relations of architects. He was devoted to St. Paul's Cathedral, where his calculations of the weight of the giant central dome and other ideas helped the safeguarding of the great rotunda by innovative concrete injections under the mighty pillars. He was a sedulous reader of the newspapers, regarded the Crown with almost Johnsonian reverence and, when his sight failed, had his family read the news to him from cover to cover. F.D.R. he regarded with scant justification as a political lightweight. Of Winston Churchill he had deep suspicions, never to be entirely lost: "a chopper and changer" politically—and far too quick in his years out of political office to demand payment for potboiling oratorical effusions in print, sometimes poor in relevance to the actual subject.

My grandmother Bessie Florence, whom J.E.D. outlived by a few months, was uncomplicatedly pious. She believed in what she called a "personal Devil." Impelled perhaps more by protective Victorian snobbery than religious principles she contrived to get her spouse made president of an approved institution near our South London suburb. This had been designed on 18th century moral lines, somewhat optimistically to reform "women of the street." The "home" was blessed with a resident vicar with the evocative name of the Reverend Stiff, which caused mirth among the inmates, a few among whom were wont surreptitiously to make obscene gestures during the church services that we from time to time attended.

My grandmother's younger sister Rosa was not much loved in the family. She chattered artlessly and interminably. I remember her telling about the early Victorian desire for social position, which Trollope was gently to satirize: how families unable to afford a pineapple for Christmas— a prize redolent with Eastern promise and social status —used to hire one for the occasion. Children were warned on no account to ask for a slice of this pineapple. Aunt Rosa was greatly addicted to a smelly old tomcat named Boots who accompanied her on her annual visit to my grandparents and left behind almost ineradicable sensory souvenirs. Boots was treated by Rosa almost like a naughty boy. She was childless, a fact which was simple of explanation: her late 19th century engagement to the Reverend George Matthews had lasted for what came to be thought far too long— five years. After the elapse of that period of reflection the two families decided to issue an ultimatum: George must really make up his mind. Did he or did he not want Rosa as a bride? The decision so forced got the couple into church but not, it seems, into bed for more than one night. "Poor George," as he was sometimes known, was a remarkably poor chess-player; clearly he failed to checkmate his wife.

On one occasion I was invited down to Uncle George's new parish Horningsham, a tiny Wiltshire village set just beside the magnificent facade and extensive park of the 5th Marquess of Bath — Longleat House — where lions now roam for the delectation of visitors. (No doubt they would have found Uncle George rather tough). Every now and then the Marquess deigned to invite his tame parson to lunch. And so I found myself at a magnificent collation in the dining room of the Great house surrounded by dazzling silver and crystal and several lackeys in livery. Lord Bath addressed me twice, as I recollect; first on some educational topic suited to a small boy; the second time to say that since I was said to be interested in pictures, the underbutler would later take me "round the House." And this was done. No doubt a far better tour than the hoi polloi get today, even after paying their not inconsiderable entrance tribute. All classes of society in the Twenties still regarded the aristocracy as something extraordinary, separate, privileged — and to some, therefore, reprehensible. As a typically deferential Victorian, J.E.D. assumed that members of the House of Lords were required merely to pay regard to an aristocratic code of their own, free from the moral restraints laid upon ordinary mortals. Responding to newspaper reports about aristocratic sexual liberties, he would merely observe, "Ah! But he is a nobleman!"

An affection, spiced with reverence, informed his attitude to Dr. Samuel Johnson. He would greatly have relished an evening with Walter Jackson Bate, a stimulating and delightful experience which Constance, my wife, and I were lucky to enjoy at Harvard. To be sure Warwick

House, the 1880ish three storey, large basemented house in Streatham five miles south of the Thames, in which our grandparents lived for half a century, was a mere mile from the site of the Thrale house with its summerhouse. Here the Doctor had spent so many agreeable and productive hours. By the Nineteen Twenties that house had gone. Part of the estate was a tennis club, and housing pressure had made the Thrale name a mere street sign. Johnson's aphorism about persons who tired of London being tired of life was quite to the taste of J.E.D. He would, on a week-end, take my sister, my brother or me round little known parts of the City of London — to the old Roman bath off the Strand, which then few knew or cared about, as well as to some of the more obscure Wren churches, including his favourite St. Ethelburga's, a very recent victim of I.R.A. terrorism.

Though music meant nothing to him, his knowledge of pictures was wide, and he admired French impressionists and Picasso. We frequently rubbernecked art galleries together. Though he never had enough money to buy really good quality antiques, he nevertheless frequently brought home interesting pieces—Japanese prints, Chinese ceramics and so forth. He never allowed his agnosticism to become public or offensive to my grandmother. Only when he was ill, practically blind and over ninety years of age did his real beliefs and knowledge of everyday expletives come tumbling out. My aunt who helped nurse him reported that, "the air was blue!" Occasionally, he had enjoyed the grand gesture: having been warned by his doctor after an attack of pneumonia to abandon smoking his pipes, he betook himself to a cliff overlooking the Bosphorus and flung them into the sea.

My mother's father Silas William Stevens was a man of a different stamp. Worldly wise, large and indolent, he had been persuaded by his wife on her second marriage that he must not lounge through life on the very small legacy they enjoyed. He should have a profession. What more suitable than the Church? So he went up to Cambridge and took holy orders as a Church of England parson. Gifted with a resonant voice and imposing presence, he was soon given one good parish after another, and in the rectory of his last parish, St. Lawrence's in Southampton, I was born in the summer of 1915. Both church and rectory were to be bombed to pieces by the Luftwaffe in 1941 and now form the site of one of the branches of Marks and Spencer's stores. (Could I perhaps have been born in the underwear department?)

It might well be held that the Reverend Silas was not right for the Church. His love of music and talent for conducting anthems together with a careful selection of pretty choirgirls gained him, it must be said, considerable local renown. And he had quite a flair for sermons. But inevitably it was alleged that he spent more time on his yacht, regularly staffed by two full-time crew, together with his four daughters, than he did in church. Everyone however was agreed on the devotion and indomitable optimism of my grandmother Susan Ellen, a Devon farmer's daughter, who spent many an hour ministering to the families of the Southampton dockers, many of whom were in stark and alcoholic poverty. Grandfather Silas died before I could remember him at all as a child.

Origins

By contrast my father's parents — J.E.D and Bessie Florence (Florrie) — are really vivid in my memory. By them, until we were of age, my sister, brother and myself were substantially brought up. The reason for this was that our parents were generally overseas, father being employed in Iraq. My Devon grandmother was an excellent housekeeper and with stout Mary, the cook, and Sarah, the parlour-maid, with their white caps and aprons, ran a very "tight ship." The menus which they produced before the First World War and after are impressive both in quantity and variety of selection. Those were the days when "followers" of domestic servants were severely discouraged, and with them their chances of meeting a husband. Half a day a week and time to go to church on Sundays were all that were usually considered adequate recreation. Perhaps this enforced spinsterhood resulted in we children benefitting in a special way from their innumerable kindnesses and good-humoured indulgence. Though very old and infirm, Sarah was one of the first to come to see our daughter, appropriately named Sarah, after her birth.

Granny Drower was a splendid guardian of her son's children. My father "Teddy" was the younger son and had been born and raised in London knowing little of the West of the country. He was at schools in Surrey and Wales, then studied law in London and became an attorney. Life for a fledgling lawyer in London, starting with little money or influence, was hard going at the turn of the century when the level of litigation was very much lower than today. Both these advantages were considered necessary, short of exceptional brilliance, for any reasonable expectations in a legal career. He therefore jumped at an offer to take a junior partnership in a Cairo firm. Egypt was then a condominium with a numerous European community to which French expatriates, such as Flaubert, had given a highly cosmopolitan atmosphere. This was to be modified substantially only after Nasser's take-over of power and the Suez Canal in the Nineteen Fifties, as well as by the later exodus of most of the Egyptian Jewish community to Israel.

Having applied himself to Turkish law, my father then moved on from Cairo to take a partnership in a firm of attorneys in Khartoum, and it was there that my mother, travelling on a journalistic assignment for a London publisher, saw him again, after a first meeting on a liner in the Mediterranean. Not long afterwards they both came back to England and were married. This took place some four years before the outbreak of the First World War. My father joined up and before long was adjutant of his regiment. After a while he was put on intelligence duties which were to bring him to New York where he was given the task of cooperating with the U.S. authorities as a member of Sir William Wiseman's mission, one purpose of which was to help persuade America to join in the war against the Kaiser's Germany. He much enjoyed his stay in New York and made many friends there.

When the conflict had eventually and decisively engaged the slumbering strength of the United States, my father was soon asked to go out to Iraq, or Mesopotamia as it was then known. He was to assist in the setting-up of an administration to be run by the British. This former Turkish province, which had known Genghis Khan, would some seventy years later see the Khan's declared admirer

Saddam Hussein. And so it was that my parents came to be stationed far from home for some twenty-five years, including those of my childhood. Every two years we children saw our parents for a few weeks in the summer, our mother coming back if possible every year.

First Assistant Legal Adviser and later Judicial Adviser to the Government, my father took part in the gradual development of Iraq to its quasi-independence in 1931, and aided the drafting of its constitution: it was still admittedly under British tutelage, which infuriated the extreme Iraqi nationalists, who were not more than aggressively vocal until the Second World War. By the Nineteen Thirties British and French dominance was widely unpopular all over the Middle East. Broken promises of speedy independence for Arab peoples made by the like of Lawrence of Arabia were resented. The poverty of many generations stood out against the increasingly publicised affluence of Westerners. When Hollywood and its cowboy thrillers arrived in Baghdad, Arab audiences were wont to cheer a Redskin attack at the top of their voices and make unwelcoming sounds when the white rescuers arrived to save the settlers. However the luxurious oriental scenes portrayed by Cecil B. de Mille were often well received —early "Dallas" no doubt.

In Baghdad before the Second World War, with refrigerators a rare novelty and the water suspect, the small European community behaved socially much as though in imperial India with bridge and cocktail parties and "club life." My mother found this tedious. She loathed the incessant chatter, gossip and complaints about servants. By contrast, to her the everyday Iraqi people were compelling.

She learned the vernacular and set about collecting folk tales from women in the bazaars and villages. These she published with considerable success, *Folk Tales of Iraq* being one such result. As a young woman she had written a series of travel romances which had brought in useful funds to help with her children's education. Later with the interest she developed in Middle Eastern customs and lore, she increasingly specialised, becoming finally recognised as an authority on the small Mandaean Gnostic sect which, at least before the Iraqi-Iranian conflict, inhabited the reedy islands of the marsh area south of Basrah. (Since 1990, contrary to gloomiest speculation as to their fate they have, it seems, been moved by the Iraqi Government to Baghdad.) My mother's unusual acquisitions and the production of a definitive Mandaean dictionary won her in late life honorary doctorates at both Oxford and Uppsala. Each year she returned to England to spend time with her children during their summer school holidays, travelling back by means of the primitive desert route by automobile to the Mediterranean coast, to Beirut, ship to Marseilles and over France to the U.K.

And so my elder sister, my brother and myself —who have always remained close — were substantially brought up by our grandparents when not at boarding school. J.E.D. used to come upstairs "after the office" and tell my brother and myself about his Victorian boyhood as we lay in our bed: sliding on the ice-covered ponds, fun with the haymakers, scrapes with the other boys of the little Devon town. London was then a very long way off in those days, though expeditions to view the Great Exhibition's Crystal

Palace originally sited in Hyde Park and then moved entire to a London suburb were a great event.

We loved to hear of J.E.D.'s travels in Central Europe. One was about a trip to Romania in the Nineties having to do with a construction contract. When he one day found himself short of money he was taken to a village and introduced to an old moneylender who promptly and without question lent him the equivalent of fifty pounds sterling against a cheque on his London bank. Some two years later the cheque arrived in the City of London for clearance. The bank sent him a photograph of it which he kept framed as a souvenir of solid British credit. He believed with old Pliny that no book could be so bad as not to offer something of value to the reader. Nor did he often travel without a copy of Horace's poems in his jacket. French literature he read avidly, though having consumed most of Proust, he solemnly took the volumes down to the bottom of the garden and burned them. Looking back, I recognise how powerful his interest in life and his gentle humanity were upon us. We thought him, as others did, supremely modest, a man doubtless with prejudices of his age, but all under control. A man without rancour.

CHAPTER TWO

SCHOOL NOTES

ince I was a bit of a noisy child, big for my age, and also to help my grandmother with my younger brother (my sister was older and less difficult to handle), a governess was recruited. Miss McGee arrived. On her bosom was a gold brooch with three monkeys upon it: "Speak no evil" and so forth. It was not that I told lies or that I manifested peculiar vices. Nevertheless it soon became clear that she looked upon me with particular disfavour. My tactics in consequence were generally to seek to outflank her where wheedling did not succeed. It came out that not so long before she had had an "unfortunate time" with a British soldier in Hyde Park, though the implications were veiled. Perhaps I represented the most repellent characteristics of the British, but that is almost to flatter a child. I could do little right. Sundry scoldings interspersed with cuffs were events inevitably out of the knowledge of my grandparents. Her behaviour became more and more condemnatory and, one day, my favourite possession, a splendidly painted railway signal, a Christmas present from my father, was used in

School Notes

vigorous chastisement which must have caused loud yells as well as a plentiful flow of blood from my head. My mother then suddenly arrived home. Confronted with this colorful evidence, she wasted no time in sending Miss McGee packing, and I was told that it would be boarding school in the near future. A couple of years afterwards, we heard that she had been placed in a home for incurables.

So, at the age of eight, an apprehensive little boy equipped with money for the porter and taxi arrived at Bristol Station in the West Country, destined for the preparatory school attached to Clifton College, where I was to spend nine years. The school had been recommended by my uncle by marriage, an Anglo-Irish soldier who had taken part in the raising of the siege of the Peking foreign mission quarter at the time of the Boxer Rebellion. He had been later posted as military attaché to Japan at the time of the Russo-Japanese War. In France, during the First World War as a brigadier general of infantry, he had astonishingly survived the loss of both legs blown off above the knee. He became one of the earliest owners of fully articulated aluminum legs. He also had a car with a clutch operated by leaning forward.

Clifton College, a mid-Victorian foundation on the lines of Rugby School, immortalised in *Tom Brown's Schooldays*, was different in more than one way from the general run of British "public" schools. For one thing it made full provision for the education of pupils of the Jewish faith. Many distinguished families in the Jewish community in Britain have had boys at Clifton. Not surprisingly music was a subject to which much attention was paid. There was very little bullying and, contrary to received lore, homosexuality was low key, if to some extent expected in a single sex situation. Nor was the school as sports-mad as some other private colleges. My coordination for ball games being evidently indifferent, I found, until I had grown too lanky, that boxing was at least something at which I could shine. Aged thirteen I wrote to my indulgent but probably bored parents that I had "just beaten Howard Smith" in the ring (that being the original name of Trevor Howard of "Brief Encounter" fame). His prancing style was distinctive and he retained it in his swashbuckling roles on screen.

At the same age, my brother and I were taken for a holiday at Bognor, a South Coast resort where King George V was taken to recuperate from a severe attack of pleurisy. Keeping, our very suitably named jobbing gardener, had unearthed an Edwardian bicycle. Keeping sported a large yellow beard, testimony to his perpetual pipe. (He was to live to be over one hundred years old and was very pleased to receive a letter of congratulation from Buckingham Palace on that achievement.) Having learned more or less to master the cycle, encouragingly named, "The Swift," I rode along the foreshore right in front of the royal establishment. To my astonishment and pleasure I saw an imposing figure with armoured Edwardian bust putting on its hat. The Queen! Gosh! Certainly an achievement which might be related with pride when I got back to school, for in the Twenties, the Cult of Royalty had been sedulously encouraged by the Establishment. I was standing, enjoying my success, when I felt the heavy hand of a Bobby on my shoulder and a gruff voice said, "That's no way to intrude into a lady's

School Notes

bedroom!" Immediate flight! Whatever physical benefit the king gained from his stay at this hitherto undistinguished resort, he does not seem to have had much liking for it. Some eight years later, when he was dying, his doctors hopefully suggested that a similar stay by the sea might be a good idea. The last royal words are said to have been blunt: "Bugger Bognor!"

Though motoring was universal by 1930 in the United States, in Europe it was a good deal slower to exercise its dominance. Only the well-off had cars to run on the dusty roads and there was much snobbery on the subject. I wrote home, "An old farmer with a scythe was trudging along a country road when he saw a motorist tinkering in desperation with his Tin Lizzie. 'Mendin' yer car?' he chirped. 'No, it's an automobile!' replied the haughty motorist. By the way, what is that thing on your shoulder?' The farmer looked up to heaven and replied airily, 'It's an automowgrass, but it won't!" Looking at letters dating from those years detailing cycling expeditions, the absence of competition from cars is now striking. But to ride through the English countryside in an open car with the changing scents of the roadside as it swept by is a glorious memory little weakened over the years.

Some of the rote learning of British education in the Twenties was not far removed from that employed by Mr. Wackford Squeers, save that there was very much less use of the cane. Some masters liked to operate a system whereby bright or studious boys leapfrogged "to the top of the class" if they succeeded in answering questions. This at least prevented deep slumber. School reports forwarded to my parents were monotonously checkered. "Could do better" was rightly interpreted to mean, "lazy!" On one occasion when I was twelve, four strokes of the cane were judged minimal retribution. But the major emotion aroused in the recipient was not repentance but alarm — old Mr. S. was clearly a victim of advanced heart disease. When he exerted himself at all his face became suffused and ominously purple. I turned round on this occasion to find him panting stertorously and felt strong guilt. What if he were to collapse and be carried off? It would be my fault. Almost a murderer! He died a year later.

Clifton had good music, and I enjoyed it fully. Grandfather Silas had been determined that his daughters should receive a ladies' education, though he found it impossible to resist seducing my mother's best friend. Mother went to a boarding school near Bournemouth, and there was some talk of her seeking a place in one of the very few university colleges for women which then suffered from the accusation that they merely produced bluestockings and were expensive. In the event she went over to Germany to study the violin in Frankfurt. There, she came across several later well-known musicians and composers including, I recollect her saying, Cyril Scott. She returned, however, and found a secretarial job with a publisher. For the next few years, London's Bohemia was where she lived and worked. An admirer, whose addresses she rejected though they always remained good friends, was Arthur Ransome, the author of children's books including the still immensely popular, *Swallows and Amazons*. Ransome was to become more famous for his part in the celebrated trial of Oscar Wilde and for his adventurous career as a correspondent in Moscow, representing not only the *Manchester Guardian* but also a powerful political point of view as to how the Soviet Revolution should most prudently be contained. When my parents returned from the Middle East on my father's retirement and took an apartment beside the Thames at Hurlingham, the Ransomes already occupied one a couple of stories above. Arthur had married Leon Trotsky's secretary. In 1946 she was still handsome in a towering way but had never acquired the knack of living in a Cockney milieu. A tremendous din emanating from the Ransomes disturbed us one evening, and I rushed up to find out what was afoot. Eugenia was booming in stage Russian accents: "Go avay! Take your vood avay' Gooooh!" What had happened was that a vendor of firewood had seized the chance provided by her opening the front door to rush in and place a bundle of faggots on the balcony in the hope that once it was there it would be paid for. By the way, Ransome loathed children, perhaps related to the facts that none had been born to the couple or, more probably, that he was too conscious that he had earned a great deal of money by writing about them.

To return to my mother and music: She owned a Klotz violin, not a particularly mellow one, but an instrument which bore the clear label of that family workshop of the end of the 18th century. She gave me the Klotz, and I began to enjoy music. When promoted rather sooner than usual to the school orchestra, which was ably directed, I was enjoined to scrape away as a second fiddle through Schubert's "Rosamunde" overture "and more," as the admen like to say. That was an enormous thrill. So too was being taken by my violin teacher to a concert where the young prodigy Yehudi Menuhin was to play Elgar's "Violin Concerto" under the baton of his mentor and friend, the composer. Denys, my brother, was less fortunate musically, if more enterprising. He arrived at our grandparents' house one day with an enormous bass tuba. It took only three days for vociferous complaints to be generated from either side of the street, and strong pressure was successfully placed on him to desist and inform the school bandmaster that that splendid instrument was not for him.

Something happened when I was nearly sixteen. I discovered books: *The War of the Worlds* of H.G. Wells and other of his futuristic concepts; George Bernard Shaw as well as Edward Gibbon's *Decline and Fall of the Roman Empire*. And I made a friend of a boy called A.N.L. Munby who collected books and possessed a remarkable collection of first editions. We used to discuss books on long walks — one of which, I still remember, covered twenty-six miles. Appropriately he later became Librarian of King's College Cambridge, holding that post with distinction for many years, but sadly dying early.

CHAPTER THREE

"ONE PEOPLE, ONE BLOOD"

At the age of seventeen, after repeated defeats in the field of mathematics, I went to Oxford to try for a scholarship. To my astonishment a small "exhibition" at Exeter College, Oxford was awarded, and this enabled me at once to ask my parents to let me abandon the narrow world of boarding school for the real one outside. The university year did not begin until the autumn, so several months in Germany were seen as a good chance to learn the language. Accordingly, I arrived at the Hook of Holland in mid-April 1933 en route for the family house of a recently retired rector of the University of Heidelberg, Professor Karl Meister, where I would be a paying guest. Spring in the Rhineland provided a scene of astonishing beauty. The profusion of blossoms, the churchbells tolling, the views from the surrounding hills of the old mediaeval town of Heidelberg —then little changed from the 18th century —left memories not easily extinguished by the shock of the brash and brutal domination of men with no respect for culture. With Hitler in office as chancellor barely a month, decrees were issuing from Berlin which disturbed, then thoroughly alarmed the academic community in that old centre of humanist enquiry. Naturally, attending the university appealed to me, so I went to a variety of lectures. In the classrooms, the Nazi students found more and more pleasure in making the life of lecturers, whose antecedents or views they disliked, intolerable by drumming deafeningly with their boots on the floor. Then, a little later, professors disappeared. Nobody dared to ask in public where they had vanished, though a nasty little rhyme circulated — a parody of a favourite children's prayer — "Lieber Gott mach mich stumm, Dass ich nicht nach Dachau komm." (Dear God, shut my mouth, so that I don't get sent to Dachau.) Traditionally, German professors had been accorded high, almost exaggerated status. This did not stop the young thugs of the local Nazi party from taking it out on the academic community. Adding insult to injury, one aggressive, cropped stormtroop bully seduced my host's elder daughter and then sent the Professor's wife an obscene message to that effect. This delightful gentleman was possessed of the surname "Himmel" (Heaven).

The Professor was determined to remain entirely non-political, something unforgivable in the eyes of the new faithful. It was nothing that in the 1914-18 war he had lost all three brothers on the Western Front. Communist or socialist sympathies would have been exceptionally hard to prove. Though Dr. Meister was cordial with all his colleagues, he had discouraged political activity as Rector, scolding the antics of the young pseudo-students who waved the Swastika or chanted communist slogans. Nor had he, to my knowledge, Jewish connections. An orthodox conservative, he saw his son Ulrich, who became a close friend of mine at the law school, join the Stahlhelm, a conservative nationalist organisation, rather than sully himself with any aspect of Nazism. Ulli Meister was to distinguish himself in the Second World War, winning the Iron Cross in Russia and finally surrendering his battered battalion to U.S. forces in Bavaria. The last I heard of Ulli was that as a Stuttgart attorney, he was engaged in defending a British soldier on some charge or other. Several friends I made at Heidelberg were Jewish who, still, a little wary of "Tommies" (the wartime epithet), were generous in keeping me generally in the picture on events unreported in the press. They told me some of what they knew about actual or suspected (read informed on) enemies of the Nazis, including a number of traditional German patriots who looked back glumly to the heady writings of Treitschke, who had lived in Heidelberg.

The rumors passing from mouth to mouth became uglier. Some professors were curtly dismissed. Others simply appeared no more. What went on in concentration camps, especially the indignities and cruelty inflicted on elderly inmates, was more and more discussed in whispers. There was that evening orgy of book-burning in the university square, carefully planned. The faculty staff had been warned that it would not be wise to be absent when the flames roared up, and were obliged to stand by while illiterate stormtroopers flung upon the burning pile volume after volume. As the Horst Wessel song was bawled out by the crowd, an officious man beside me told me that it was an insult not to stretch out my hand in salute; I did so

"One People, One Blood"

without delay thinking (as later experiences proved wise) that live dog is better than dead lion.

Such was the academic scene. But in that first year of Nazism, the face of most of Germany still remained much as it had been since the Middle Ages. In Mannheim, close by, was the old 18th century opera house familiar to Mozart but since pulverised by Allied bombs. Close by was the baroque Schloss of Schwetzingen, now site of at least one major annual festival, with an excellent restaurant which used to, and probably still does serve delicious asparagus and omelettes. Automobiles were few, and walking was pleasant in the hills in Baden and along the banks of the then comparatively unpolluted and bathable Neckar. After a while I joined a group of Wandervoegel (wandering birds) run by an indomitable explorer, Professor Brecht-Bergen. We paddled canoes down the Rhine, the Rhône, and Main and cycled through two thousand miles of Southern Germany, visiting that astonishing series of walled and castellated mediaeval towns such as Bamberg, Rothenburg and Wuerzburg, all as yet untouched by bombing. We camped as a rule. Each member of the party carried on the back of his or her cycle a portion of a kind of military beduin tent, which when set together, was divided in the middle with the girls on one side and the boys on the other. It was all very decorous, and my first real experience of girls. The roads were frequently unmetalled; a few horse and ox carts formed the means of transport for villagers. On one tour of six weeks, I spent just over five pounds sterling in all. A year later, Brecht-Bergen was put under pressure by the Nazis to "affiliate" with the Hitler Youth, which he refused to do and ceased the operation of his Wanderbirds. We were possibly among the last of this species, born in the Twenties to the naturist enthusiasts of a better, healthier Fatherland.

Touristically, Heidelberg had long been depicted as a playground for student princes and handsome wenches with blond pigtails. There were certainly a few orchidaceous young women and handsome young fellows about who danced the tango superbly so tourists were not too disappointed. The latter would have been ignorant of what was going on that year. Already Richard Tauber, the Viennese tenor, who had won immense popularity in Germany as elsewhere, was feeling pressure from the Nazis— the Third Reich would not be the "Land of Smiles." If joining a local stormtroop was fulfillment for many workers who had long been unemployed, particularly odious was the social snobbery which caused some Germans with a "von" to their name to seek to be taken into the more select S.S., offering immediate social prestige and, more unpleasantly, the heady ability to frighten. Just one week before the Second World War started, I sat with a friend in the Berlin Schiller Theatre with a gentle, intelligent young executive working with the Bechstein piano manufacturing company. My sister had met him when she stayed as a paying guest with his family some years before. He loathed and despised the Nazis and all their works, and no doubt it had been hard to disguise this. As a consequence, he must have been under observation. After 1945 it was rumoured that after the invasion of Russia, he was drafted with others suspected of lukewarmness into one of those units destined for most dangerous assignments from which few were expected to return. But to return to the theatre: on my immediate right had settled a powerfully built man in stormtrooper gear, who from time to time cast a scowling, penetrating glare upon my friend and myself. During one interval, he suddenly turned to me and asked, "Are you not frightened of me?" — a question which made the answer, "Why should I be?" sound ridiculous. But at that moment, one felt transported swiftly and disconcertingly away from civilized Western life, as if suddenly set upon the moon. This brush with brutality, one felt, was one unassailable reason why Fascism and Nazism in particular had sooner or later to be fought to a finish.

There were more satisfactory occasions in pre-war Germany to remember. One evening in 1935, I was in Heidelberg sitting in an open-air dance bar on the lower slopes of the Koenigstuhl above the floodlit, old castle. The band was playing a sleepy tango when a cheerful, young American decided to exercise his right, which elsewhere would be unchallenged, to "excuse me" and dance with a particularly attractive girl who was partnered by a Nazi, to judge from his badge. The latter was furious, demanded that the American should abandon his impudent pretension and then actually challenged him to a duel. This caused his "rival" so much astonishment that he broke out into loud laughter, whereupon the Nazi was obliged to retire to the glee of not a few onlookers. Several of the old Prussian and traditionally exclusive Student Corps, who tended to look down on the Hitler enthusiasts, maintained their tradition of duelling with sabres. They offered a curious but nauseating early morning spectacle as, on a signal, they slashed humorlessly at each other. Their faces and necks were mostly padded, leaving the area of the mouth and jaw unprotected. The object was, one was told, to receive a wound which could be kept open for some while by the judicious use of salt by the surgeon, leaving a scar to be worn, like a tattoo, perpetual proof of valour.

German Student Corps held from time to time what could only be described as a militarised beer orgy, drinking steins of beer to the barked command of a student who called himself a "Drinkingmaster." I went once, returning nauseated by the spectacle of these vomiting, young heroes. Certainly an enormous amount of beer was drunk in Heidelberg by students and visitors alike. Amid the alcoholic fumes, I witnessed some grotesque scenes: a famous pub in Heidelberg is still the "Red Ox" in the main street of the old town. There with my friend Ulli late one evening, we noticed a black student engaged in conversation in English on the other side of the saloon. Shortly after a large American, presumably from one of the Southern states came in, ordered his stein of beer and began to drink. But then he caught sight of the black man, ordered him off the premises, and when the latter rejected this suggestion, hurled his mug at him across the room with a crash.

So in September 1933 I was back in a homeland I had heard sneered at as effete. To be sure my next three years were those of a most unheroic Oxford undergraduate. It was an institution in many ways still mediaeval—clerical discipline reigned little changed from a century before. Attendance at chapel was compulsory in most colleges; a

"One People, One Blood"

rigid curfew system applied, a kind of university police, directed by an athletic don assisted by burly runners, swooping on offending students, especially those in Oxford taverns, and those late back into their colleges. Women were excluded after eight o'clock from the mens' colleges. They were accepted, it is true, by three colleges of their own, but it took several decades to see them given places actually within mens' colleges. Undergraduates were treated rather like senior schoolboys by the more old-fashioned dons. So some tended to behave as such. Practical jokes were still thought screamingly funny. Someone let a greasy pig run amok in Exeter College's quandrangle. The Prince of Wales when at Magdalen College was said to have enjoyed a jape where he and a friend, leaning out of a window close opposite to him, sent filled jerrypots sliding down a cord simultaneously from both ends with the consequent explosion timed to douse a don walking underneath.

More subtle and satisfactory was the fooling of dons in their senior common room by Frank Harley, a friend of mine who indicated at long distance that "she" was a nun who might be prepared to recount the dreadful indignities which she had undergone in the Spanish Civil War. Eagerly accepted, she was well-dined and then proceeded to tell the goggling audience her tale, suitably lubricious. It was simply an astonishingly successful rerun of that old chestnut "Charley's Aunt"— in both cases unfeminine feet and a glimpse of trousers were eventually to give the show away, but in Frank's case not until he was well out of the college and about to board his train for London.

Odd characters abounded at Oxford in my day. One ancient don was universally known as "the Crab" from his habit of walking sideways, very fast. A posse of enthusiasts met annually by the Martyrs' Memorial in the town center to bewail the 17th century fate of the luckless King Charles I. There were also strong and wholesome characters like the rector of my West Country college, Exeter. Dr. R.R. Marett was a distinguished anthropologist and regarded by all as a splendid fellow. On one occasion a college servant ("scout" in university parlance) came to him obsequiously, tendering a condom which he declared he had found in one of the undergraduates' rooms. The Rector is reported to have taken it out of its packet, blown it up and to have boomed joyously, "Ah! A balloon!"

In those days Oxbridge was looked upon by the better-off sections of British society as a gentlemanly means to broaden and mature the mind of young men, of seeing to it that they acquired general social airs and graces, that they could converse intelligently on a reasonable variety of subjects — more of a finishing school concept. There were some undergraduates — not in my college — who were hardly ever seen in lecture rooms, who preferred to hunt, row on the river, paddle punts down the delightful Cherwell, frequently throw sherry parties (gallons of this liverish liquid must have gurgled down undergraduate throats in my time) and have expensive lunches with their friends in the Oxford restaurants. People like that were well-provided with funds. By contrast there were a few scholarship students who attempted not only to survive on their emoluments, but even to send money home to their families. For them life was very hard indeed, and they must have left Oxford with a degree of resentment. As compensation, they usually did extremely well in the final examinations.

There is no question but that present day students in all universities in Britain—and there has been a proliferation of higher education colleges in the last two decades especially— are far more serious and intelligent in their studies than we were. Nor would today's university authorities tolerate the lackadaisical attitude to scholarship which was then not uncommon, and which I certainly shared. Today places are precious and students who do not "make it" get thrown out to make room for others. It was expected that I would read history. But the old don who taught it in my college seemed grotesquely narrow, prejudiced and anachronistically antifeminist— he grumblingly objected to women in his lecture room! The prospect was so unappetising that I asked, and was grudgingly accorded another syllabus. Instead I plumped for what was then sometimes looked down upon as a newfangled hotch-potch— PPE, or Modern Greats, composed of politics, philosophy and economics in that order.

There were several dons in this faculty who became well-known later. One of my tutors was Frank Pakenham, later Lord Longford, a polymath Labour peer devoted to the improvement of man—who refused to believe what I told him about Irish nationalist smuggling of supplies to German submarines in the First World War—tales I had heard on the Atlantic coast of Galway. Another was Kenneth Wheare, an international authority on Federalism. A bright young don at Christ Church was Richard Crossman, who became a key figure in Harold Wilson's administration in the Sixties. I must have sat close to the latter in lecture rooms since he too graduated in PPE, a contemporary. Obviously a slovenly and thoroughly unsatisfactory student, I dodged lectures, preferring to argue in the Oxford area pubs (an illegal pursuit) and left my essays until the last possible moment. The Film Society committee was much more to my taste and Hollywood, the UFA studios and French productions became much more compelling than Kant, Adam Smith or Bishop Berkeley. Moreover London, in those days when there were plenty of fast trains, could be visited and enjoyed in the space of an evening. Not surprisingly I left Oxford with a bad degree but with an opulent fantasy acquaintance with screen stars, some superficial knowledge of old English churches, a little skill with a punt pole, scraps of international politics acquired during vacations on the Continent, a soupçon of French and a distinctly livelier interest in girls.

A vast range of student societies proliferated, first among which was the Oxford Union, with a large debating hall, a good library and a reasonably priced restaurant. Though I became a member of the Union as a matter of convenience, the playing at national politics and aping of Members of Parliament which went on there and in the various party political clubs served to put one off. So did the notorious motion, passed just before I came to Oxford, declaring that the Union members would no longer "fight for King and Country." This well publicised decision predictably infuriated large sections of the middle classes and encouraged mightily those Nazis who were convinced that Britain would be a walk-over. What was not generally

"One People, One Blood"

realised was that much of the assenting vote was motivated less by detestation of war—though pacifism was strong—than by general dislike of Winston Churchill's arrogant son Randolph, who noisily led the opposition to the motion.

Several Americans, with a sprinkling of Rhodes Scholars, were at Exeter College during 1933-1936— my three years at Oxford. They included a delightful Virginian, Harry Lee, whom we used to implore to "keep on talking" in his rich Southern tones. He went later to Charlottesville to teach English. There was also an Ivy League sports-car enthusiast named Phipps with an inseparable buddy Don Tatum, both of whom seemed made of charm and money. Another was a silent, impressive anthropologist— Dr. Gluckmann I seem to remember—who was a good deal older than the rest of us and kept to himself. Among German Rhodes scholars, there had been two or three years earlier at Christ Church Trott zu Solz, executed later for his gallant part in the resistance against Hitler. A talented Rhodes scholar at St. John's College was Fritz Caspari, who sought academic freedom in North America after 1939 and who was to occupy a high post in the German Foreign Office in Bonn postwar.

Oxford was just the place to get to know something about girls. Not the "undergraduettes" as a rule, many of whom were dowdy— Harold Laski's niece Marghanita being a much sought after, lively exception. Various attractive dons' daughters were about beside the belles of Oxford city and beyond. There was Valerie, a starlet from the Elstree Film Studios. She was beauteous but unacquainted with the rigidities of London etiquette. We had arranged to meet in town on a Sunday, but in those days about the only outside amusement available on that day was a visit to the zoo, then flourishing. However, only members of the Zoological Society were that day allowed in. So I telephoned an old Middle Eastern acquaintance of my father, Sir Percy Cox, whom I knew to be a member, and asked for two tickets. He readily agreed and it was arranged that I call to pick them up next Sunday morning. Sir Percy was a highly distinguished pillar of the Raj who, in retirement, had taken a fine apartment overlooking Kensington Gardens. His consort Lady Cox was formidable. Like Oscar Wilde's Lady Bracknell, she possessed a bosom of salient splendour upon which might have been set a loaded tea-tray. Junior staff in the past had been said to be terrified of her imperious social demands.

Valerie and I met as arranged and repaired to Knightsbridge to fetch the tickets. More than a little uneasy lest Valerie encounter Lady Cox, I ascended alone to the third floor and was received— Sir Percy himself resplendent, as always, in a frock coat, stock with gold pin and pale salmon waistcoat. "And where is your companion?" I was asked. Told she was below, Sir Percy himself at once insisted on fetching her upstairs. A minute or so later the two appeared. Valerie lost no time in chirruping to Lady Cox, "Oh! You do have such a sweet butler!" The zoo visit took place, but some weeks later I received a jaundiced letter from my father, pointing out that he had just had a communication from Sir Percy expressing the withering view that, "in my opinion your son seems to lack discipline."

"One People, One Blood"

In shaming contrast my elder sister Peggy (Margaret S. Drower) applied herself steadily at London University and graduated with much distinction. She was later made Reader—that is to say deputy head of faculty—in Ancient History at London's University College. During the Second World War she worked as executive assistant to Freya Stark, that extraordinary writer and traveller in the countries of the Middle East who quietly organised groups of people friendly to Britain at a time when Nazi German ambitions in that area were at their most dangerous. Freya Stark died very recently aged one hundred years.

As for Denys my younger brother, he chose Cambridge and after the war began an interesting and varied career with the B.B.C.

CHAPTER FOUR

MEETING THE JAPANESE

In those days of high unemployment, such a lack of achievement was no way to secure a job at the Foreign Office which temperamentally attracted me. So, when by chance someone mentioned that the Japanese Embassy was looking for an English secretary, I at once applied, was interviewed and landed the job. My chief was Shigeru Yoshida who, after World War II, was so highly regarded by General MacArthur and served as Liberal Party Prime Minister for a number of years. The ambassador was an understanding and generous boss. My duties included sitting in his more or less reserved seat in the Distinguished Strangers' gallery of the House of Commons and reporting to him orally on the character of debates of particular interest to the Japanese. I was in that seat at the time that Anthony Eden resigned from the Chamberlain Cabinet in 1938. Next to me was a gentleman with an American accent who asked various questions about procedure in the House and who was who, its composition, procedure and so forth. He then revealed himself as "Joe Kennedy," the new American Ambassador to the Court of St. James's.

The drafting of letters to people in the United Kingdom for the ambassador to sign was naturally a regular duty. At that time the Japanese military had begun their deliberate attempt to overthrow the Chinese regime using what was generally and correctly alleged by the Left as great brutality and mendacity. So the replies required to deal with protests began to include the Archbishop of Canterbury and other church leaders, community representatives and other persons showing growing distaste for Japanese conduct internationally. In the Embassy there was a remarkable amount of infighting on various issues. Yoshida defended me steadily against the allegation fostered by his Minister Baron Tomii that I was a "plant" by the British and that I should be ejected. I learned willy-nilly a certain amount of Japanese, though (not surprisingly) without encouragement from the Embassy staff. Several of the younger secretaries had been to British universities, and I remember the brilliance of one young attaché named Kase, who later became Chef de Cabinet in Tokyo and is recorded in the filmed version of the 1945 Japanese surrender on the deck of the "Missouri," half-concealed by a vast black top hat.

Certain of my duties were social rather than political. At one dinner where several influential persons were being entertained, sashimi was served, together with other Japanese specialties. I already fancied myself as someone not entirely incompetent with chopsticks. Alas, my portion of sashimi, which always tends to be rubbery and elusive, did not easily yield to efforts to divide it into mouthfuls.

With a sudden flip, a large piece flew across the dining table to land in the lap of the Master of Semphill, a pillar of the House of Lords who, as one might imagine, pretended that nothing whatever had happened. It was also expected that I should play golf from time to time with the staff, the game only recently having been taken up in Japan. In a cupboard I still have a small silver cup acquired in an Embassy competition. The post was certainly unusual and quite interesting, as I was paid on a scale commensurate with that of a Foreign Office Third Secretary, but clearly it was not something which could offer any kind of career. Naturally, when Japan teamed up with Nazi Germany and Fascist Italy I resigned and soon after went to the North of England, having found a job in industry as a sales department trainee in a large soap manufacturing firm.

Yoshida admired Churchill and, like him, affected a large cigar. He was also clearly a man of strong character. Though he certainly shared the desire of the Japanese governmental establishment for a Greater Japan, based at least on an extension of imperial influence on the Chinese mainland, he opposed the methods of the super-nationalists. He was increasingly, one knew, under pressure from the Japanese Navy to modify his critical attitude towards their policies in Manchuria and China. Letters and telegrams bombarded his office, some declaring him a traitor to the Emperor. Yoshida was not intimidated by such missives. Nor even when an infuriated admiral sent a signal announcing his early arrival at the Portman Square Embassy to beard the ambassador in his den. Yoshida took no more notice of this than of other abuse and threats. So, when the admiral marched into the Embassy foyer one day at lunch time shouting, "Here you are! I demand to speak with you!" Yoshida swept past him, cigar at a perky angle, declaring, "I'm not available!" Shigeru Yoshida was probably fortunate to escape with his life during the Second World War; for a time he was held in house arrest.

Between 1933 and the outbreak of war in Europe, I several times returned to Germany, a land where things were rapidly becoming so different from life in Britain. There was an underlying brutality of outlook which Georg Grosz has so vividly portrayed. The Nazis promulgated contempt for the English gentleman and his snobbish and outdated ways. Golf was sneered as a game merely for elderly drones. London clubs were full of effete reactionaries with too much money. As for New York, the fashionable young men were degenerates, one and all.

In Berlin, as in other cities, the hyper-inflation of the early Twenties was fresh in people's minds; it still lingers. Much of the middle class had been rendered indigent. In restaurants, one still saw doggy bags filled, not for pets at home, but for later consumption by their owners. Foreigners were evidently more numerous than Germans in the more expensive establishments. Many families, like my friends in Heidelberg, were glad to supplement their incomes by taking in foreign guests. Anything which promised to make life easier and more like the old imperial days held attraction for them. Until the outbreak of war in 1939, life continued on the surface almost as normal. Nevertheless, the organised looting of Jewish shops shocked many Germans themselves. But it was still possible in 1935 to visit, as I did on several occasions, the small Jockey Club by the Kurfuerstendamm, a night club where the friendly and brilliant pianist was named Kohn. I established there an interesting contact with a senior officer cadet of the Naval Academy in Berlin, who used, he said, to climb out of the building at night. Like so much of the traditional German defence establishment, he was contemptuous of the crude ideology, the catch-penny programme, the scuffling by Nazi bullies in the drinking shops and the grotesque anti-Semitic propaganda. An attractive and able young fellow; I have often wondered what became of him.

To some extent the top characters in the Nazi hierarchy succeeded in presenting a personal image of ability, even bonhomie. Goering's wedding in the spring of 1935 to a large actress was used to depict him as a jolly, full-blooded bridegroom. Immense crowds swarmed round the Berlin cathedral. The ex-King of Bulgaria "Foxy Ferdinand" drove by, a practical joker released a large stork which circled over the newly married pair with Goering flashing rows of what the crowd called "tinsel" on his paunchy frame.

To many observers from Britain and the United States, it was hardly credible that so much of Goebbels's propaganda could be so totally and immediately swallowed by persons one might otherwise have thought reasonably percipient. A supposedly eminent Berlin academic spent time one evening explaining to me the importance of the stars in the fortunes of a greater Germany. One had, he declared, only to noticed the effect of the moon on both women and tides to realise the power of stellar influences. The night before the German-Soviet pact was announced, my mother and I were at a reception given by the World Congress of Archaeologists, to which she had been invited. In our modest hotel was a middle school head-teacher who obviously swallowed lock, stock and barrel all that appeared in the Nazi newspaper, *Voelkischer Beobachter*. A secretary from the British Embassy had at the reception whispered to us the news of the signature of the Pact, stressing the grim consequences to be expected. Accordingly we rose early for breakfast, concealed the headlines in the worthy schoolmaster's newspaper and laid it on his plate. When he descended the stairs we timidly suggested that the Soviet regime might always be in the eyes of the Hitler Government most infectious and dangerous. This produced the expected lengthy diatribe against Stalin and all his works and the firm conviction that the Fuehrer would never, but never have any truck whatever with him or his gang of murderous ruffians. We then quietly ate our breakfast and waited for him to open his lurid *Beobachter*, the expected splutterings ensuing *prontissimo* most satisfactorily. But urgently advised by the Embassy by telephone, we packed our bags and left for home by the next train. Poland was to be invaded almost within the week, and the War in Europe began.

CHAPTER FIVE

ANOTHER KIND OF JAPAN

Already enlisted as a "territorial" (volunteer reservist) in the artillery during the months after the Japanese Embassy experience, I found myself in the Liverpool area a private soldier almost at once. Earlier that year, the training course offered by the soap producing firm I had joined required a spell in the factories of the North West of England. In those days, there was a very considerable difference, economic and social, between life in the South of England and in the Black Country and textile towns of the North. The Liverpool area, with its heavy Catholic immigrant population, had (and still has) special problems of poverty and unemployment.

Finding a welcoming and thoroughly delightful farming family to stay with close to the factory was good luck. They became firm friends. The farm atmosphere was in kindly contrast with the dreary industrial installations and the pervasive reek of whale-oil and other fats used for soap and margarine production. I joined a group of Liverpool voluntary social workers organized by a bird-like, courageous little lady, Miss Keeling, a pioneer who organised small loans to families in trouble, offered advice and so forth at a time when social services were rudimentary. The spectacle of children without footwear, filthy, stunted and generally Dickensian, was an education for someone who had enjoyed a privileged education and middle class comforts. There was great poverty. Some parts of Liverpool were dangerous and avoided by the police whenever possible. One of Miss Keeling's most successful helpers was a gaunt person in black bombazine and tall black bonnet straight out of a fashionbook of the Eighteen Eighties. Fearlessly, she would clamber up stinking stairways and demand part repayment of a previous loan from a ferocious tough, reeking with drink, near whom very few of the rest of us would have ventured.

Ireland is "just across the water," and in the early Thirties, life in the South was primitive. With friends I had been over to Ulster from Oxford during a vacation. We were amazed to find how mediaeval the views of the Protestant majority were. Nothing seemed to have changed in essence since the 17th century Battle of the Boyne. And in the South there was little toleration either. On the magnificent March-gale tormented Atlantic coast of Sligo, Galway Bay and Kerry, we found ourselves among people living in turf huts, with cattle on one side of a peat dividing wall and the family "higgledipiggledy" on the other. Radio had barely arrived in the hamlets. We walked several miles on pressing recommendation to pay a call on a schoolmistress who owned a wonderful phonograph with no fewer than seven records of Irish dances to all of which we, of course, listened. On two evenings in succession, we were invited to a barn dance. Both nights nearly turned into day as we capered round the earthen floor, the girls perspiring in the candlelight with a tatterdemalion old fiddler sawing away with apparently inexhaustible energy. One villager, who gave us "pads" for a shilling the night, together with his wife, sought repeatedly to "get off" his daughter with one of my German companions. The latter would suddenly find himself alone with the girl, who was admittedly pretty but who would not have found Munich city life very easy.

As a trainee in the Liverpool factory complex, I spent time in the various departments seeing how soap was made, packed and distributed, how accounts were organised, the wonders of the Hollerith machine — the punch card predecessor of the computer — and went on selling expeditions through the countryside. Some towns, such as Hull on the northeast coast, had ferocious reputations as the graveyards of commercial travellers. Selling to suspicious tradesmen was certainly no easy matter there, and one suspected a kind of subtle revenge when it was demanded by the shopkeeper that before any business could be done, pelmets advertising soap powders and the like be affixed forthwith to large and awkward old-fashioned shopwindows. A Belgian fellow trainee had a thoroughly alarming experience when undergoing instruction from the men in the "soapery." Ingredients were pumped into twenty ton capacity vats and superheated steam soon brought the contents growling and boiling up near the top of the vats where paddles were wielded to test the texture of the mixture. My colleague must on one unlucky day for some reason have allowed his attention to wander, for within a trice, hideous quantities of boiling soap rushed up and out of the vat creating panic and derision.

The Wirral, where the factory is sited, is now covered with houses and adjoins Liverpool's sprawling suburbs, but it is also close to North Wales. It was delightful to be able at the weekend to drive my minuscule Austin Seven —bought from a fireman for fifteen pounds— to the green valleys and mountains of that pleasant part of Britain. The vendor brought it to the farm, every brass component shining, little bigger then a perambulator but just right for a young bachelor with no motorsport pretensions. My farmer friend, having made one or two caustic observations, allocated a part of the henbarn as garage. The little car enabled me to drive down to the main company offices in London where advertising was next on the training menu. One time, I decided to stay the night on the way down. There were no motorways (though Hitler was completing UBahns rapidly all over the Reich).

At about six o'clock in the evening, I turned east off the main road to find a village and soon came upon one. There was, someone said, a bed to be had just down by the church —a certain good lady occasionally put people up. So there I knocked on the door and was given a little room and an excellent "tea," with ham and eggs. As I was finishing my food, there appeared a cadaverous old man who addressed me in sepulchral tones as follows: "Do you ring?" As the church clock was at that moment striking, his meaning was clear enough, so I artlessly replied, "Yes." "Quarter to ten!" he growled and disappeared, leaving me with an increasingly uncomfortable realisation of the foolhardiness of my contract. Never had I tugged at any church bell before, though I was aware of a tale popular among campanologists about a luckless inexpert ringer being dragged up to the ceiling where the bell-rope disappears on its way to the bell. Next morning, accordingly, I walked to the church and into the forbidding belfry. Recklessness now took over, and I heaved away at every bell rope in the tower making the most appalling "tohubohu." After ten minutes, when my arms were half out of their sockets, the old man came in, gave me a steely look of disapproval and announced, "That's enough!"

The service was about to begin. The congregation was composed of the wife of the parson, the verger and myself. Two psalms were gabbled through by the parson, his wife repeating them half a bar later, so to speak. Altogether Alice in Wonderland might have been expected to join in. There were no hymns and, mercifully perhaps, no sermon. After the war, I looked for the village, the name of which mysteriously had vanished from my mind. I never found it.

In September 1939, I was back in the north of England and the "phoney war" had begun. My territorial artillery regiment was mainly composed of middle-class volunteers, but we had a fair proportion of very rough Liverpool types who despised washing and were nearly always in some sort of trouble. Since I was large, my first job was to help our regimental military policeman escort Gunners Murphy and Sweeny down to the "glasshouse" (military jail) in Somerset, to which they had been sentenced for a month for a series of non- or misappearances on parade. The trip down South necessitated a long journey. The train conductor accordingly kindly arranged for us to share his cold tea, if not his sandwiches. Both our charges were at first truculent and totally disrespectful of the armed forces. All the same this bravado markedly diminished as we approached the dilapidated and dank 18th century prison which has since, I'm glad to note, been somewhat improved. By the time they were handed over to the bustling "screw" (jailer) they were very silent indeed. All in vain, the spell in the glasshouse did little to improve their military acceptability, and they were soon transferred to some freshly constituted unit which dug holes and built embankments.

I was really quite sorry to see them go. For a pint of Guiness stout, I had written letters designed to cheer up their girl friends and salute, in a more sober way, their legitimate spouses. It was sufficient. I was informed to write, "Dear Wife" in the case of the latter. But one could give it a whirl with girl friends: "My sweet darling" was very O.K. for Maggie; "My treasure" for Janey. It was not too surprising to learn that when they were eventually transferred to their new unit, a sizeable group of keening women were seen waving goodbye to them on the station platform, the farewell group doubtlessly including their wives.

At the start of the 1939 war, there was next to no military equipment in reserve in Britain. Nearly all had been sent over with the Expeditionary Force to France, and practically all that was to be lost at Dunkirk. Accordingly, we amateur soldiers were obliged to train with imaginary guns and imaginary guntractors, feeding illusory ammunition in imaginary military situations to our ghostly implements of destruction. That winter proved abominably cold. I was not fortunate, like one or two of my comrades, to have a girl friend to spend time with in the sentry box when selected for guard duty, often my lot since I was tall. The proverbial army scrounger/comic Good Soldier Schweik made an occasional appearance, though his techniques as related in that seminal book seemed rather sophisticated.

By the spring of 1940, I had been shortlisted as a "potential officer," my candidature not unassisted by a brief success against a miner in the regimental boxing competition. The colonel was said to have "noticed," and soon I was off to an artillery training centre at Aldershot near Windsor. As this was quite close to Sandhurst, the crack infantry cadet school where my brother was — he had joined the Coldstream Guards —and we were to see something of each other. Soon he would be in North Africa with the so-called Desert Rats —the Eighth Army —locked in struggle with Rommel. The summer of 1940 was a pretty melancholy period: the Blitzkrieg crashed down upon the Allies over in Belgium, and the strategy and morale of the French military were rapidly exposed as useless. Every day radio and press reports grew blacker. By the time I received a commission as a second lieutenant France had collapsed, many of our troops had been rescued, though without arms, and German parachutists were expected to descend in our midst every night.

Meantime the War Office had formed an Intelligence Corps seeking linguists, and I was informed that this, rather than an anti-tank gun unit, would be for me. In between various interrogation technique courses, I studied

Another Kind Of Japan

German and French military terms, carried out depressing reconnaissances of the coast of Eastern England—pathetically devoid of any solid defences —took part in exercises, sometimes using as headquarters crumbling mansions of penniless aristocrats. German bombers from time to time made hit and run raids along the flat coast, killing more cows than people, but reminding us of how pathetically stretched were our resources, how tenuous in hard terms were our chances. Waiting either to invade or be invaded was soul-rotting. Then came the order for me to repair to a depot in Oxford preparatory to embarcation for "somewhere." German was not likely to be used, that was plain; evidently my rudimentary Japanese now might have to be developed for somewhere where it might be of some use. Could that mean anywhere other than Singapore or Hong Kong?

Half a dozen supposed Japanese interpreters accordingly found themselves on the liner turned troopship "Capetown Castle," which left "for an unknown destination" at the end of June from Glasgow. Several in our small group of Japanese speakers really had a good knowledge of the language, including a former missionary who was very amiable. The others, who were also quite fluent, had been in Japan as commercial representatives. My own knowledge was, by any comparison, paltry.

The voyage was comfortable enough for officers; the other ranks had a much less agreeable time since the conversion to troopship had been hasty and incomplete. Our lumbering convoy expected trouble, and we made a wide detour, almost to Iceland, to avoid submarine attack. In this we were successful, though opposite Spain, long range Focke-Wolf bombers tried their luck. No ship was hit, and we continued down to Capetown where a row of delightful young ladies were waiting on the quayside to entertain us. One of my fellow interpreters, an Irish Guardsman, was grabbed as we disembarked, and I too was taken along, benefiting from his handsome presence. During the refuelling weekend we saw much of the Capetown area, were presented to General Smuts, the respected former opponent of the British during the Boer War, and became aware of the gap, social and economic, between white and coloured inhabitants. The views of some of the Africaaners on Nazidom and race were disturbing. Later of course their support for Hitler became positive and, with the formation of a declaredly pro-fascist party, the division between many of the Afrikaaner and English settlers opened anew.

The voyage to Singapore had its moments. When we proceeded into the Indian Ocean, the sea extraordinarily phosphorescent, I had my camp-bed set on the deck at night. The vast twinkling expanse of tropical sky, swinging majestically with the ship, was something not easily forgotten. Soon we were dropping anchor in Bombay. I had heard that my mother was likely to be somewhere in India. A telephone call made clear that she was in fact staying in Poona in the hills not far from Bombay. So a telegram from the kindly governor brought her to the jampacked Victorian railway-station in Bombay, and we were able to spend half a day together. She told me that my father was in Palestine, intent on making use of the time before he could return to his desk in Baghdad by setting himself to learn Hebrew.

Another Kind Of Japan

My parents had undergone a rough time in Iraq. In the Spring of 1941 there had taken place an Axis-inspired revolt by a group of Iraqi officers. By the beginning of May they had marched into Baghdad and invested the British Embassy. Rashid Ali, their leader, asked for help from Berlin but was disappointed only to be sent a small contribution in gold. If the British were sluggish, despite the staging post importance of the Habbaniyah airfield, thirty miles away from Baghdad, the response of the German command in North Africa was half-hearted. British civilians crowded into the compound of the British mission. The United States Minister, Paul Knabenshue, nobly received the overflow of some 130 of our passport holders. My father stood sentry for several nights with rifle and bayonet inside the American compound. Something like a modern siege of Lucknow ensued, while a relieving force was put together by Cairo headquarters. Habbaniyah was recaptured in short order, Baghdad relieved and most British residents flown out with their wives to Palestine and India. Not much news of the coup was published in Britain while I was still awaiting embarcation. However, the War Office had let me know my parents were safe.

My mother could now give me details of events in Iraq, of how lucky everyone had been to escape a massacre. As it was, she and other women waiting on the airfield for a plane to take them off were obliged to shelter from snipers by climbing inside large concrete drainpipes. We had lunch with the Bombay governor and his family, impassive Indian servants in white attending, man-operated punkahs moving to and fro to provide some coolness in the hot season. A delicious curry followed. That and the ice-cold jellies served next remained teasing memories when hunger succeeded a few months later when I had become a P.O.W. In the afternoon, we went down to the Willingdon Club, run on old colonial lines but allowing, on the insistence of a recent liberal governor-general, a proportion of Indian members. This was my last chance to see either of my parents for more than four years.

One can now reflect that Rashid Ali's abortive revolt might well have changed the whole course of the war in the Middle East. Subsequently, the coup manqué seemed to have been almost entirely forgotten. But one might safely assume that Saddam Hussein, then a boy, took good note.

Colombo was the next port where the "Capetown Castle" put in. Several of us hired a car and drove up to Candy, the capital which was later the headquarters of Lord Mountbatten's staff. We were able to spend the night there, and amid the gleam and flicker of crude torches, witnessed the great sacred procession of One Hundred Elephants, the heavily decorated animals swinging their trunks, the dancers whirling, the pipes and the drums and the swirling incense-laden, thoroughly intoxicating fervour of the occasion. Then back to our troopship and, within a week, the awaited landing at Singapore, close by the muzzles of the big guns.

For the Western popular press, Singapore was a fortress with impregnable defences. It did not take long for the truth to become apparent to someone on the spot that those vaunted defences were few, scattered and largely out of date. As to the last point, only one or two British units seemed to have a full realisation of what jungle warfare in the 20th century meant. Colonel Stewart of the Argyll and Sutherland Highlanders was a driving man who voiced contempt for the tactics he guessed would be employed by units he considered had gone soft in the tropics. Deemed a Tartar by his own men, capable of ordering them out on a further route march just after they had arrived back from a day's exertions, he found when the time came that they would stand by him to the last. A full-scale command exercise a couple of years before had shown that a determined invader could make pretty easy inroads by landing on the east coast of Malaya and pushing down south, landing on Singapore Island and taking most of the defences of the island in the rear. But not much had happened since. The reasons for this were various: it was most unlikely that the home country would be in a position to send out much equipment, since Britain still faced a sea-borne invasion. There were other military priorities— the Middle East in particular. Malaya could wait. Nor could more troops be expected from Australia, where a noisy lobby was already hostile to further involvement in Malaya. As for the governor of Singapore, he was not at any time prepared to see his citizens made "human sandbags" in any conflict which, in later years, might prejudice the return of Britons to the territory. Looking back, the governor had much sense on his side.

So Singapore was substantially a military bluff. A well-known American radio correspondent was as eager to display this to the world as Malayan Command was keen to impede him, and something like a battle of wits developed. Just before Pearl Harbour, with the Japanese effectively in control of Thailand, the Thai military attaché asked to visit the coastal gun defences. It was accordingly decided that I should be in the escorting group with senior artillery officers. It had been hoped to leave him with the impression that the fixed emplacement guns (which, contrary to popular legend, could swing round 180 degrees) were of seventeen inch calibre. Imagine one's consternation when one gun barrel he looked at with particular attention bore, near the breech, the clearly painted legend "16 inches!" However, we learned subsequently that the Thai officer had signalled his home base that an attempt had been made by the British to bamboozle him into believing that the guns were only sixteen inches in calibre, not, as he was pretty sure, seventeen. So we were cleverer than we knew.

Working by day in Malaya Command Headquarters, I lodged in a small summerhouse in the garden of one of the big colonial houses of a predominantly European residential area. Fruit bats hung like bunches of swart fruit in large trees overhead and one evening, when I gave a small cocktail party, they bestowed profusely and embarrassingly unwelcome gifts upon my guests. A Chinese school teacher came from time to time to teach me how to write Chinese characters, using the traditional inkstone and brush. I had a Hailamese servant named An Ah An, who was polite, efficient and always available when required. He proved a loyal friend: one day, after the surrender, I had been sent with a party of prisoners to bring to the camp meat from the Singapore Cold Storage Depot and had been allowed by the Japanese corporal in charge to go and buy a few cigars in the market. The market was crammed at that time with Chinese, Indians, and Malays. Bending over, looking at bundles of little cheroots, I felt a gentle but insistent prodding in my back. Something was pushed into my hand. I turned, saw that it was a ten dollar bill and just caught sight of good An Ah An disappearing into the throng. When I got back after the war, I tried to find out what had happened to him. Nobody knew for certain but it was generally agreed that, as a friend of the British, he had paid the penalty.

It was about four o'clock that December 1941 morning when the roar of aircraft and boom of bombs announced the beginning of the war in the Pacific. I wrote home, "The old familiar noises-the obedient jaga (nightwatchman) hurried to turn on all the lights. When they were turned off again, he instantly flooded the place with light. This comedy having been played some three times, a naval commander and myself had to sit on his head..." But one felt from that time on a numbing sense of inevitable doom. The bluff had been called with a vengeance. How long would we be able to hold out?

Somerset Maugham jibed that when he arrived in Malaya, he understood the shortage of housemaids in Britain. Perhaps, not surprisingly, when I had applied at the main library for a copy of Maugham, the woman at the desk looked firmly at me and said, "We don't care to stock works by that gentleman." His literary reputation did not matter. He had been a cad—had abused the hospitality of various up-country planters just in order to make a good story. No doubt the majority of the British in the peninsular had wives who were barely interested in any book, still less in the lives of the brown people around them. Sexual mores were affected by heat and boredom, but, on the whole, their menfolk were hard-working and honest, and many had given time to become volunteers in the local Defence Regiment. They were later to suffer terribly as prisoners of war since most were not of commissioned rank. The rubber plantations where many of them held jobs as overseers or plantation managers were ready means of infiltration by a well-trained enemy, supplied in advance with maps based on the work of resident photographers who had surprisingly frequently turned out to be Japanese.

Enough has been written about the Malayan campaign following the Japanese landings on the east coast, about the disastrous dispatch of two of Britain's heaviest warships without air protection on a vague brief to intercept reinforcements, about the rapid air superiority by Japan "O" aircraft and the destruction of the sixty odd planes —mostly of obsolete design—which were available on the first day of the conflict. It was certainly true that lecturers on the fighting forces of the Japanese beforehand had been briefed to say that Japanese pilots were likely to be incompetent. Supposedly there was some deficient mechanism in their head which prevented them from flying upside-down, utter nonsense I had in fact refused to promote. Very soon the Japanese were nearing the large causeway which separated Johore from Singapore Island. The governor had argued long and with conviction that to mine that entrance to the island before hostilities might break out would merely panic the population. So what preparation for destruction was eventually put in hand offered little obstacle to determined, trained invaders when the plungers were pushed to explode charges.

Another Kind Of Japan

Headquarters life became increasingly futile. I went up-country one day with the British General Officer Commanding, General Percival. The map was changing every hour, and very much to our discomfiture. He himself had risen as a staff officer rather than as a fighting man. With his large topee, thin legs and lack of chin, Percival was a far from reassuring figure at a time when Montgomery-like leadership, infectious dynamism and sturdy purpose were needed desperately to inspire the troops. Amid the confusion caused by rapid enemy infiltration backed by tanks, a number of units, both British and Australian, undoubtedly fought gallantly with heavy casualties, but that could not be said of others, green and easily demoralised by the new warfare methods used by the Japanese. Meantime, a whole division of British troops was about to land at Singapore; most were from the eastern counties of England; none had been trained for tropical warfare and certainly not for jungle combat. The diversion of these urgent reinforcements from the Middle East theatre of war had been last-minute and political. Australian governmental threats to reduce cooperation generally had again been made and not particularly obliquely. Their own general in Malaya had proved an awkward customer with more of a flair for personal publicity than military achievement. So, many of the 18th British Division hardly stepped off their troop transport than they were "put in the bag."

Now the Japanese were pressing so near it seemed bizarre to continue to sit in the operations room with those tell-tale pins on the wall-maps adding to the pervading pessimism. So I asked that since I was a trained artillery officer, I might be sent to take the place of a casualty. This was agreed and posting to a volunteer regiment based near London followed. By melancholy coincidence, I discovered that I would be in the shoes of a former cadet whose bunk in the officers' training unit the year before had been quite close to my own. An enemy shell had blown him to bits.

CHAPTER SIX

"YOU OUGHT TO BE DEAD!"

The artillery regiment to which I was posted, the Hertfordshire Yeomanry, proved welcoming. Morale was high, thanks to an intelligent, driving cotton-broker of a colonel. I was given four 25 pounder guns and told to get on with it. The Japanese were starting to cross the causeway in large numbers, and we were seeking to make life as unpleasant as possible for them. But soon in danger of being isolated and surrounded, we had to pull back a couple of miles. I was posted as forward observation officer that very night to keep watch lest the Japanese seek to outflank our men by coming round the huge oil tanks situated by the naval base which had now been evacuated. Before leaving, the navy had set these tanks alight, and they were sending enormous sheets of flame high into the air, casting an extraordinary light all around. One felt a new sense of total isolation with the surrounding semi-jungle expectantly neutral, but no Japanese attacked the position that night. We then moved from position to position, with Japanese fighter aircraft flying overhead unchallenged, shelling and being shelled, though moving back all the time to the city of Singapore. The men were shaken by the Japanese use of new-type bombs which made a very loud noise but were, in fact, physically less harmful. Our last emplacement was a Chinese school near the Serangoon Road. Here, we heard about the casualties being suffered in the city. We were near the end of the siege. After two days more, although we were receiving an anticipated frontal attack by the Japanese infantry who were pressing on in other parts of Singapore Island, we were getting alarming reports of a breakdown in morale among some Allied units, with drunken looters reeling through the streets and dispirited men searching for their units. Sniping from a few houses nearby picked off one or two men in my battery. Then a dispatch rider came to say that a surrender had been arranged. The war was over, and we were the first Western prisoners of war to be taken en masse in any modern conflict in the Orient. History would hardly excuse, one felt, a military defeat of this size. Bluntly an enormous and shaming SNAFU which Churchill now had to recognise.

I had been sent out to Malaya, supposedly to interrogate Japanese P.O.W. In the whole of the two month campaign, only six had been taken up-country. Truculent and obeying the Imperial Rescript forbidding surrender to an enemy, they had resolutely refused to say anything. Now, perhaps, what slight knowledge I had of the language might prove of some use. Having (against the enemy's surrender orders) destroyed our guns, the colonel released me from "considering myself under close arrest," his penalty for my having organized an escape party. In reality, the odds on getting back to a secure Allied base were vastly less than many of us imagined. Some did make it to Sumatra but were again seized by the rapid Japanese overrunning of that part of the Dutch East Indies. It was good afterwards to learn that one major at headquarters did indeed succeed in getting himself and several men near the coast of Ceylon, where they were picked up, rowing by turns in an open boat for many days, practically waterless under the searing sun. Very few others escaped roving Japanese patrol vessels. Some were picked up by fishing craft and then handed over to the victors in hope of reward.

Philip Toosey later became a fast friend in camp conditions, and I fully forgave him for obeying the special instruction he had received from Percival as a part of surrender conditions—that officers should stay with their men. This was a novelty to be sure, for King's Regulations instructed all ranks to do their utmost to escape in the event of being held captive. But looking back there is little doubt that since officers were permitted in most cases to remain with their men, until about a year before the Japanese surrender— mass breakouts being then thought possible by the Japanese high command—P.O.W. morale was kept far higher, sickness reduced and many lives saved. The Japanese from time to time suggested that officers should be on their own; there would, they argued, be less pressure for officers to perform physical work. That was patently disingenuous, and we opposed it on principle. Our fairly honest reply was that life for our guards would be easier if we were there to maintain a discipline over the men. No commander of P.O.W wants trouble of any sort if he can avoid it.

"You Ought To Be Dead"

The realities of capture began with a sixteen mile march to Changi on the eastern side of the island where there had been an airfield and barracks, and which now of course is the site of the international airport. Over fifty thousand British and Australian troops then sorted themselves into unit groups without help from their captors who were jubilant and to a degree bewildered by the vastness of their prize. A few of our officers were perfunctorily interrogated, but that was all. There was really rather little for the Japanese to find out. All the same, if it had been my lot to be questioned, I would have been careful to conceal, as throughout the years of imprisonment, that I had ever been an employee of the Japanese Mission in London. The military would have concluded at once that I had been a spy, which I had never been.

Orders were promulgated in quantity that we should "sincerely" obey every instruction of our captors. In gratitude for his extraordinary magnanimity, we should honour the Emperor by guarding ourselves—the principle of group responsibility would be widely applied. Rations were at once reduced to the absolute minimum. Cockneys found a plain rice diet doubly unsatisfying— both novel and unpalatable. Malnutrition soon made its appearance, and various tropical diseases—beri-beri, dysentery and malaria began to pick off the weakest.

I returned to the headquarters group, where help was needed badly in translating for formations who could not speak a word of Japanese. Prisoners were coming in all the time, picked up from various parts of the peninsula. One enterprising Scots youngster got hold of a steam-tractor and, for a couple of weeks, blarneyed his way about outside the perimeter, picking up food from friendly

Chinese and water and coal from dumps controlled by the Japanese soldiery, pretending to be on official duties for his captors.

Within a couple of months, parties of prisoners began to be sent under guard to presumably distant destinations out of the Changi camp. Appointed interpreter to about one thousand Australians, I was lucky enough to find that they were volunteers, many of whom had fought up-country under Colonel Charles Anderson with remarkable gallantry at a critical part of the campaign. Anderson, with whom I worked for much of the three and a half years of captivity, was an exceptional and coolly imaginative man who was awarded the coveted Victoria Cross and eventually held a seat as Country Party Member of Parliament for New South Wales. He was expert at that kind of verbal bridge where your opponent holds all the coloured cards, and you have a few twos and threes. All the time with the Japanese we would be obliged to negotiate, procrastinate, plead, haggle and, where possible, steal in order to make life a little easier for our men.

After a traumatic voyage up the island-studded western coast of Malaya in an ancient Japanese tramp (sunk soon after by a British submarine) with the men so crowded into the hold that they had to take turns to lie down, we arrived at the little port of Tavoy in Lower Burma. Thankfully off the ship, we marched to our first assignment—the enlarging of the airport. About a dozen of the men made off, hoping to escape north; they were intercepted and shot. There were hutments already there which had been used to house the airport construction coolies, and we were to occupy these for the next few months, during the very heavy monsoon. The Japanese sergeant with whom

"You Ought To Be Dead"

we had to deal was a decent enough fellow and, on one occasion, took me up with him on the back of an elephant into the market in Tavoy and let me buy cigars and blocks of palm-sugar for the troops. Quite near the camp was a small Buddhist monastery; there the ponggyis in their saffron robes occasionally whispered words which we supposed might have been those of encouragement, but we certainly would not have trusted any offers of help so far as evasion was concerned. Sometimes at night, we could hear the gongs and the whining drone of the Burmese oboes coming from a *pwe* (popular entertainment) in the distance.

Then we were again transhipped up the west coast with its myriad jungle-clad islands, anchored at Moulmein, and were marched into the town square and told to settle for the night in public view, presumably to rub in the discomfiture of white men. But that night we were smuggled a note containing a friendly, sympathetic message from the mayor. Next morning, when we were moved south in the direction of the jungle, a crowd of Burmese surrounded our ranks throwing little cakes, blocks of palm sugar, cigarettes and cheroots in such quantities that our guards angrily forbade any more to be picked up. It seemed that already the Co-prosperity Sphere was not totally appreciated.

After some hours we arrived at a clearing where there were several huts: bamboo with palm leaf covering and long split-bamboo sleeping platforms. These were our quarters at this first staging camp of the construction of the strategic Burma Siam Railway. We now found that nearly all our guards were not Japanese but impressed Koreans, whereas at Tavoy we were under soldiers of the Guards

Division which had been so successful in Malaya. Many of these unwilling Koreans— forbidden to speak their own tongue on duty— hated the Japanese bitterly but were conscious that there were stool-pigeons in their ranks. Predictably some took their frustrations out on the prisoners. One or two in each group of guards could be counted upon to be horrible; occasionally, a kind guard would confide that he was a Christian—and several were helpful in a variety of small ways. The non-commissioned officers were nearly all Japanese.

One thing that struck us strongly was the considerable command responsibility expected. Whereas in the Allied Forces a group of, say, two hundred P.O.W. would have been placed under the charge of an officer, the Japanese had sufficient confidence in a corporal. Industrious, they were extremely good at improvisation. They expected us to be too and on several later occasions, we marched to a supposedly "good camp" to find that it was a mere point in the jungle and that we were expected to set to work at once to build our own hutments, irrespective of whether it was in the middle of the day or night, and of the weather conditions, which often meant steady torrential rain, unkind to men with recurrent malaria or worse.

In few armies is it usual for really competent officers to be placed in charge of prisoners of war. Certainly, with only one or two exceptions which might have been accounted for by some feud or scandal, the quality of the swaggering, drunken types who held our fate in their hands was deplorable. The doctor in charge of the health of several thousand P.O.W. was known to have no more than veterinary qualifications. The worse the conditions, the more frequent the exhortations. It was repeatedly

"You Ought To Be Dead"

rubbed in that we should be ashamed to be prisoners. We ought, they declaimed, to be dead. The Japanese Army never surrendered. In their allegiance to the Emperor, they had taken an oath to that effect. Westerners were incurably lazy, arrogant and impudent—we would be properly sorted out! Many a time, I had to translate these homilies to groups of our men; it was not hard to learn that particular phraseology. Lapses of discipline in the Imperial Forces were, we were frequently (and undoubtedly correctly) informed, punished by a clout on the head, if not worse. One Dutchman, at a later stage, suffered repeated brutality because it was alleged that he sneered at his captors. The fact was the unfortunate man suffered from a facial defect which could have been construed as a grimace.

My efforts to explain this merely resulted in my being given some of the same treatment. Interpreting was a precarious undertaking: if one had to report something intensely displeasing to one's captors, the odds were high that a beating would ensue. Since I stood well over six feet, tiptoe swipes were usually to be expected. Being much taller than the Japanese or Koreans was not a good thing. For centuries in the Far East, the humble had been supposed to keep their eyes, and indeed their person, low before their betters. Nobody was allowed in mediaeval Japan to look down from a window upon the passing noble. Sensitiveness about race coupled with this deep-rooted tradition demanded an extra element of "submission" which was not always easy for our less sophisticated officers, and several times I had to mistranslate in order to avoid retribution. A pitfall for anyone attempting to speak Japanese is the marked differentiation in grades of speech which should be employed. When, for instance, addressed by them in the coarse vernacular, my reply, to officer or indeed to any of our captors, had to be in the honorific mode. Never having received formal language tuition saved me from one disastrous pitfall at least. A near disaster of this type befell a later friend, Phil Foisie of the *Washington Post*, who had been trained at a language school in California and who was instructed to interrogate a group of Japanese P.O.W. on one of the Pacific Islands, the first time prisoners had been taken in any quantity. The first prisoner was brought before him and asked the usual questions. He appeared extremely embarrassed, showing this by an ill-suppressed snigger. The same happened with the next man brought in. By the time my friend was attempting to deal productively with the third P.O.W, he felt obliged to ask him what was wrong. It then became plain that my friend, a firmly married man, had been using women's Japanese. His language tutor had been a woman.

The main task for the working party under Anderson was to prepare a railroad track and lay sleepers and rails which, together with simple metal chairs, had been captured. The purpose of the railway, which was ready for use a few months before the end of the war, was to form a reliable means of communication between the Japanese forces operating in Burma and along the Indian and Chinese frontiers and the Gulf of Siam. Our men had to work at least eight hours a day and sometimes a good deal longer. At first, no rest day was allowed. Then, as the Japanese came to see that exhaustion and illness worked against them, a Sunday rest was permitted. It was a constant battle for our tireless young medical officer to succeed in keeping sick men from having to go out to work, which would be likely to drag their frail health further down. To a remarkable extent he succeeded. But with a diet of coarse rice, and an extremely low protein and vitamin intake, together with an absence of mosquito nets, recurrent malaria was the inevitable lot of nearly all.

Cholera struck other working parties with whom we had brief contact as we worked further south. One camp was so affected by this water-borne disease that, at one point, there were barely enough men with strength to bury the dead. The corpses were roughly piled up and burned with brushwood. Cholera is a terrible disease. The speed with which it desiccates a man is reminiscent of medieval descriptions of plague—in reasonable health in the morning, dead by nightfall. When eventually it struck our camp, the Japanese, fearful for their own skins, quite quickly brought in vaccine, the effect of which may have been as much psychological as biological. Anyway, it put an end to that epidemic.

Our guards and their officers were eager to be treated by as well as to benefit from the knowledge possessed by our doctors. Frequently they asked for injections. No medical officer to my knowledge misled them as to the character of an injection he administered, but several medical orderlies, knowing how very low our stock of medicines was—we scarcely received any at all from the Red Cross—did inject water instead of the capsule the guard might produce. One Japanese lieutenant, Naito, was in the judgement of our doctor very likely suffering symptoms of tertiary syphilis which the injections he demanded would hardly be likely to help. His behaviour, at the very least, had to be considered unpredictable. One evening I was on my "bed" and feeling poorly from an attack of malaria. A message came via a guard that I was to attend him at the camp headquarters. I replied that I was ill and asked what was needed. The guard made off and soon came back saying that Naito demanded my instant presence.

At his office, it was at once clear that he was half seas over. What he really wanted was boozing company. An unpleasant night followed: by turns aggressive and maudlin affectionate, he rambled on about men being like cherry blossoms which fell from the tree and were trampled underfoot; how glorious it was to die for one's country and especially for the Emperor; how all the P.O.W. in his charge, having made such a disgraceful surrender of their military responsibilities (a little truth in this, I felt) did not deserve the magnanimity of the Japanese people as displayed in their being allowed to work for the glory of Japan, etc. He was well supplied with bottles of the local "jungle-juice"—a ferocious type of hooch concocted in the Burmese villages which, on an empty stomach only too recently scoured by dysentery, was a form of hospitality one could have done without.

More gratuitous was the sword flourishing which began about midnight, the gleaming blade whistling close over my head. The drunker Naito became, the more he pressed brandy upon me. My expedient, hardly novel, was to tip as much as possible down the leg of the bamboo table. Temporary success in this ploy ended as dawn approached. He suddenly noticed a pool on the earth floor. So....he had been insulted and deceived. A cunning look transformed his features. To the hospital compound not far off a sailor from the "Prince of Wales" battleship had been taken a few days earlier with tell-tale smallpox bubicles all over his body. Eureka! the illness I had pleaded was quite clearly that same dread disease. Military hygiene now required that I must join the patient forthwith. The latter was not, of course, provided with any bed as such, but was lying on a bamboo platform, covered with large bluebottles which were enjoying the pus from his sores. The prospect was not encouraging.

It was promptly considered appropriate by the Korean guard, one of the less cooperative, that I at once should take my place next the patient. Few could have been more grateful to that old Dr. Jenner and his vaccinating enthusiasm. To be sure, choking throat infection ensued, but that was all, largely thanks to the assiduous kindness of the orderly, a young blond artilleryman from the Dallas area known in the camp as Tex McLeod. He smuggled in some medication and a bit more food and certainly saved more than one life.

Beside being such a good friend in need, Tex possessed a gallows sense of humour. A day or so later, the camp "horse-doctor" arrived, having presumably been advised that a small-pox epidemic was expected. He looked cursorily at the patients and then hastily withdrew, demanding that he should be provided with a bowl of disinfectant. Just before his arrival, the orderly had just finished swabbing the open pustules of my companion. Instantly, Tex offered this very bowl, and we observed with macabre relish and anticipation the thorough way in which our captor washed his face and hands in that disgusting liquid. Sometime later the Japanese colonel in charge of railway P.O.W. paid a state visit to the camp. Perhaps Lieutenant Naito had been "shopped" by one of the non-commissioned Japanese or perhaps his bizarre conduct had made itself known in other ways outside. Whatever the reason, he disappeared as soon as we had made our way further down the track and we never saw him after that.

Meantime, there was nothing for it but a stay for two weeks in the isolation compound as a smallpox suspect. A former coal-miner from the north-east of Britain joined us, I forget now why. What is clear in my memory is the difficulty— at least at first— of "getting the drift" of his North Country dialect. It must have been extremely hard for men like him, coming from tight, introspective communities, to be transported to the tropics and then given a diet totally strange and inadequate for health. He told me of his very hard life at home when the welfare state had been a dream of political idealists. Provided with poor physical reserves, he was to die before our eventual release. And on another occasion a young Cockney prisoner told me that before he joined the army he had "never been sure of two meals a day at home." Now, at least, he commented, his captors provided them to some extent. It was easy to realise the support which men like him would give on return home to any political party offering the electorate a full programme of social reform. The famous Beveridge Report, providing the framework of a welfare state, became known to us in outline via the B.B.C. No wonder Churchill failed to gain re-election in 1945.

As we laid track and moved over the malarial Three Pagodas Pass—the frontier between Burma and Thailand (the pagodas turned out to be mere runts a few feet high) sometimes marching or packed into railcars, we passed or joined other groups of prisoners, British, Dutch and a few Americans like Tex who had been captured with their guns in Java. There were so many Dutch that we formed a joint P.O.W. "command" in the largest camp, beside the River Kwai of film notoriety. The task there was indeed the construction of a sizeable bridge for the railway. Though three Japanese interpreters were now available —the other two being real linguists—there was a constant succession of "incidents" and misunderstandings which needed explanation.

One morning in 1944, very large Allied bombers flew over our camp, obviously intent on destroying the Kwai bridge two hundred yards away. Unfortunately, negligible damage was caused to the structure, but the bombs destroyed several of our long hutments. So later the tally of P.O.W. was found to be a round dozen short. We argued to steady Japanese disbelief that nobody had run off, that it must be that the missing men had been blown to atoms. Predictably, the Japanese insisted that there must be visible remains and that men had escaped. In fact, one Indies-Dutch prisoner, who could easily pass as a Thai, did make his way out of the camp, which was merely surrounded by a small bamboo fence, and hid in a village a few miles away, where he stayed hidden until the end of the war. So far as is generally known, no white P.O.W. in Thailand got away from captivity for any length of time with one exception, a British soldier Corporal Pagani — who is still alive. Certainly none was able to regain an Allied fighting unit. This was not quite so on the mainland of Malaya, where three or four Allied soldiers, who had been hidden by Chinese irregulars, were successfully picked up by a British submarine.

That unsuccessful Allied bombing raid, which provoked delighted P.O.W. cheers (immediately suppressed by our captors) is also strong in my memory since at that moment I was in the headquarters office. I ran outside and jumped into a one-man air raid shelter pit. At once, it became evident that it was already occupied—by a speckled snake. Neglecting the whistling of the bombs, I leaped out pronto.

Morale has been mentioned. The making available of credible earthly hope to sick and exhausted prisoners was of the greatest importance to our devoted medical staff. I fear the promise of eternal life reiterated by the official padres, Catholic and Protestant, was of substantially less effect than a confident assurance that officers might make that the war was being won and that one day, not too far off, the troops would get home to their families and jobs. We were fortunate to have among our numbers brave men who secretly built, maintained and operated small radios throughout our captivity. To listen to enemy broadcasts was absolutely forbidden. In one Dutch camp—where a clandestine radio was not adequately protected from discovery—several officers who operated it were slowly beaten to death in front of the rest. Among our group of P.O.W., a Tasmanian engineer, Arthur Watchorn, who has lately become well-known as an international yachtsman, made a most ingenious radio in a water canteen in such a manner that when the top was removed water only could be seen.

Colonel Charles Anderson early decided that the policy should be to restrict tightly the circle of those with knowledge of B.B.C. broadcasts, and of the means of their reception. Nevertheless, news in some vaguish version might be provided to all ranks under a time-lag. This would enable some form of credible explanation to be given to our captors in the event of a leak: that we had heard such-and-such from a local, met during worktime outside the camp. The waterbottle radio, however, did not go on forever, and it was found necessary to construct another, using batteries smuggled in by a friendly Thai trader who was after the war recognised gratefully by the British Government. This apparatus was hidden by setting it under a certain ledge in the deep and friendly camp latrine.

An awkward problem was naturally the transport of any radio from camp to camp. A solution was found unexpectedly by the Japanese camp commander's having demanded one or two prisoners as personal servants. They would tuck the set into his personal baggage just before departure, thereby ensuring that it would never be subject to search. They also stole Japanese newspapers for me, which I endeavoured to make out in the secrecy of the latrine. If surprised there, disposal would have been simple. After Hiroshima and Nagasaki, when Allied parachutists entered our camp, the Emperor having called quits, Toosey caused astonished mortification on the part of the camp commander by offering him mock thanks for having so safely transported our vital means of news of the outside world.

Searches, either by the camp staff or by the Kempei military police were quite frequent. One afternoon, I was called to a Dutch officers' hut where the Korean guards were already searching. Imagine my horror when I noticed lying distinctly on one bamboo and gunny-sack bed a compass! Pocketing it fast seemed to offer dubious chances of success. So I waited in trepidation for the guard, who was not very bright and named "four eyes" from his powerful eyeglasses, to discover such flagrant contraband with subsequent dire consequences for more of us than the negligent Dutchman. "Four eyes," however, picked up the compass, put it to his ear, shook it a few times and pronounced, "Nogood watchee!"

At the River Kwai camp came orders for men to be selected to go to "very good camps" in Japan. Some spent some days in Indo-China en route. It was there that Pierre Boulle, the French author of *The Bridge on the River Kwai*, was said to have obtained the key theme of his book. Imagination seasoned with artistic license produced the plot that a British P.O.W. colonel became so determined on making a fine job of the bridge that he opposed the destruction of it by his own side. There was a slight element of truth in this scenario: Charles Anderson, a New South Wales farmer of proven extraordinary bravery, was sometimes under criticism from one or two less intelligent fellow officers for seeming on occasion almost prepared to cooperate with his captors. Such critics argued that P.O.W. ought to refuse to "work for the enemy" and, if they were absolutely obliged to, for instance on the Kwai Bridge, they ought to do as bad a job as they could get away with. This underestimated our captors and was poor psychology, Anderson replied. Men should not be expected to be sophisticated; they must be able to think that what they were doing was up to a point worth-while. His duty, in the absence of any reasonable prospect of either individual or mass escape, was to give his surviving men the best possible chance of getting back to their families short of military collaboration, which he would without doubt have rejected absolutely and at once. To say to his men that they should work badly would do little harm to the Japanese. Their response would doubtless have been indiscriminate brutality and an immediate reduction of rations — already low enough in all conscience.

CHAPTER SEVEN

LIBERATION-SUDDEN AND SWEET

As mentioned, probably for fear of some troublesome action by P.O.W., all officers were eventually removed to a separate camp, where they were to see the end of the war. The Japanese colonel in charge of this camp, Noguchi, was particularly arrogant and unpleasant. It was late in May, 1945 that I incurred his violent displeasure when I was reported to have rebuked a Korean guard who was taking it out on a water-carrying party without any cause whatever. Perhaps unwisely I had said to this particular guard that there was such a thing as the Geneva Convention (to which, of course, I knew the Japanese had originally refused to accede but might now perhaps, with defeat looming, find it politic to recognise in some way). Somewhat to my surprise, a summons to Noguchi's office was followed by a savage tirade, and a hefty beating up in the course of which I fell over his writing desk and broke it in pieces. The Emperor had been insulted. To make amends, I was accordingly to be thrown into solitary confinement "forever," This sentence turned out to be some eighty days until the war suddenly ended.

The first week or so of my imprisonment were spent in a crude, narrow, underground air raid shelter, very low, so that I became quite friendly with the chikchak lizards which walked upside down along the earth roof. I was woken one night by a rat nibbling my foot. Then a "change of scene" into a cell next to the guardhouse. I did not know what was happening to my comrades. For their part, they nobly did their utmost by request and protest to lighten my condition if my release could not be secured. The cooks, all officers of course, did what they could to help by secreting broken up vitamin tablets in my daily riceball, which probably saved my life. So there I stayed until the atomic bomb, to which presumably I owe some debt of gratitude, brought the Pacific War to its dramatic end. By then, malnutrition and blackwater fever had made time of no importance. Vague memories linger of the doctor and other friends breaking into the cell and hauling me out. Another few days, they said later, would have made their action of little use. Noguchi's record was later to be deemed generally abominable and he was eventually hanged by a War Crimes Tribunal in Singapore.

It was in that guardhouse cell that I realised, as others have so often done in similar circumstances, the reserve value of an extended and liberal education. The hallucinatory realism of the plots of books and films I had liked or been gripped by; amateur dramatic parts once taken; walks through Germany, Austria, Italy and France and, of course, the British Isles all occupied my thoughts. Concerts conjured themselves up where I imagined playing the violin; singing in a choir—especially Handel. It seems that the guards afterwards reported that I annoyed them by singing. Probably this was the reason why, on more than one occasion, they threw into my cell large, rattly centipedes which I could not see, but which saw me clearly enough to give me hostile and extremely irritating bites.

Officers who had parachuted from the Special Task Force 136 were the first to bring the camp news and comfort. Food and medicine airdrops followed, one of which killed a cow. Heady days, which now seem a whirl to my friends who survive. The kindness which was shown to my sick comrades and to me was indeed overwhelming, as we were now given the latest drugs, tasty American "K" rations and transported from one form of medical care to another. The Chulalongkorn Hospital in Bangkok remains a delightful memory, though marred by the raving of one of my comrades who had typhus, from which he recovered. Here, our nurse was a charming Three Umbrella princess— that is to say, very blueblooded.[1] She was also so pretty that we voted to have put off the threatened arrival of a team of British Red Cross nurses from Rangoon, who we ungallantly presumed would be redfaced and beefy. But when they did arrive they were charming, and we understood that a psychologist had decided that we were suffering symptoms of having been far too long away from home! Hard to forget though was the handsome eggshell blue jar filled with deliciously fragrant jasmine blossoms that our Thai angel brought into the ward. The jar was a present too, and I kept it for many years. Like

---

[1] The more umbrellas, the bluer the blood!!

most of the aristocracy of Thailand, she was a highly accomplished dancer, and when Field Marshal Slim (as he later became), the commander in the region, visited the hospital she and friends gave a display of Thai dancing which he, like us, found quite delightful. It seemed that when the Japanese had taken over Bangkok the well-born ladies of the city had taken refuge in hospitals to avoid the attentions of the soldiery.

Life in Bangkok in 1945 and the general composition of that ancient city itself were still elaborately unchanged from those of many centuries. Ridicule and giggling resentment had greeted the initiative of the pro-Japanese dictator Pibun Songgram who, in 1941, had issued a decree that all good Thais ought to wear hats under pain of his displeasure. This had predictably followed closely his takeover of the main hatmaking factories. As someone unkindly sneered: "Collar and tieland!" When somewhat recovered, I was invited to dinner by one of my princess's friends. The servants still observed the old Thai decorum of moving about gracefully on the floor— a species of decorous crawl— handing round the dishes and drinks with traditional deference to rank.

My father, I was told, had asked that I be permitted, when fit to travel, to go back home by way of Iraq where he and my mother had previously returned. So it came as a pleasant surprise to be told by General Slim that he was posting me to PAIFORCE, the British army centered on Baghdad. In consequence, I was enabled to spend five most interesting months there, my duties being theoretical for the most part, requiring mere reporting to headquarters every month. An unusual invitation formed more or less a part of these obligations. Our general in Baghdad summoned me to dine with others in the company of the Soviet Minister, of whom he had suspicions, no doubt well-founded; the idea was to make the Minister drunk in the hope of interesting revelations. This ploy, however, did not work. The Minister, saying nothing whatever beside the blandest generalities, took us bumper for bumper until we could hardly sit in our chairs—so game, set and match to him!

The railway from Baghdad to Aleppo was then still operating, and I used it to visit the north of Iraq. Our consul in Kirkuk, with whom I stayed, took me out for a picnic one evening to a part of the terrain where there was a great amount of oil. He demonstrated an explanation of the Burning Fiery Furnace by scratching a hole in the soil and lighting it with a match, it being then possible to fry food in a pan! I met some of the Yszidis, so-called Devil worshippers, in the area north of Mosul and toured the Iranian frontier where the Kurds predominated and where Suleimaniyah formed the main community. The mutasarif (mayor) was specially hospitable, offering his guest a gargantuan meal of mutton and rice and making very clear his intense dislike of the Iraqis in the south. He put me up in a house in which in the early morning, strange swishing sounds were audible. Looking out of the window it was evident that it had rained in the night. Now many of the inhabitants were engaged in rolling their mud roofs flat to prevent their disintegration.

Staying in Baghdad was a fine chance to get to know my father, who had inevitably been a rather distant, though benevolent family figure. He had early acquired a good knowledge of Turkish law which had helped to assure him his job at the Ministry of Justice. Old Turkish ways of thought were hard to die: one British judge who came out to adjudicate a series of cases before the Iraqi courts had been had been mortified to learn that the bazaar-centre of news and comment counted him an uncommon arbitrator: "They say he gives back the bribe to the party who loses!" But already, barely sixty-five, my father was showing signs of years spent in intense heat, unmitigated by air-conditioning, together with dicey water and far too many tiny cups of coffee, necessary concomitants of any form of discussion with Arabs. An excellent golfer, who won the local golf club cup on several occasions, he had done his best to keep fit. But the climate is unrelenting, and when he returned next year to the U.K. on retirement, he was already seriously ailing with kidney trouble and he died pretty soon afterwards. It was good that his services in Iraq had been rewarded by a British knighthood. He would certainly, like my mother, have been depressed though not too surprised at the way events have turned out in Iraq over the last decade.

CHAPTER EIGHT

BACK TO THE EAST

In March, 1946 came orders home for demobilisation. The flight from Iraq to Egypt with a refuelling stop beside the Dead Sea preceded a couple of weeks in Cairo at one of the permanent British barracks. Moved by anti-British nationalism, when things had looked black for the Eighth Army three years before, some shopkeepers hopeful of favors from Rommel's troops entering the city had placed "Welcome Germany" signs in their windows. Now, with new Muslim fundamentalists fanning nationalist flames, anti-imperialist feeling was fizzing and isolated incidents involving British soldiers were being reported. One afternoon someone gave me a seat in his Jeep into the city centre to look around the bazaars. We were obliged to reverse smartly by the sight of a cloud of missiles hurled in the air by crowds of slogan-shouting demonstrators. Things were to be far worse a few years later when there was a full-scale riot directed at the British. Shepheards Hotel, long regarded as a British social headquarters, was burned down and the Turf Club, together with a number of its habitués, suffered the same fiery fate.

Despite the kindest of "welcome backs" from members of my family at Southampton as I descended the returning troopship's gangway, England seemed chilly and inhospitable. I had served the Crown. To return to work for a board of directors was unattractive. True, my job had been kept open, but I knew that a salesman's career was not for me. Britain, exhausted by two world wars, was now reform-minded to be sure, but gray and apologetic. Physically, so many buildings were either seedily decrepit or a pile of rubble, certainly in the main cities. Rationing seemed to apply to almost everything, and I was not too sorry when in the summer, having received my civilian hand-out flannel suit and final discharge from His Majesty's Armed Forces, the Foreign Office offered me a job in Indonesia, then known as the Netherlands East Indies. This would be on the information and publicity side at the British Consulate General in Batavia Jakarta. I was getting back upon the horse that had thrown me.

There was still a war on out there. The Dutch believed they had an undisputable right of return. They would continue their rule as colonial masters. But the Americans were cool toward this ambition and had done little to facilitate it. Though the Japanese in the last days of the war had given independence to the Indonesian nationalists, their motives were highly suspect. The British Government were much in two minds. They were not keen to encourage a situation which might soon infect their own position in Malaysia. The Dutch, furthermore, had been allies in the fight against Hitler and Japan. Naturally, it was frequently urged in Europe that Holland ought now to be supported, whatever means were adopted to restore her overseas power.

On the other hand, for years pre-war international observers had been less than enthusiastic at the way the Dutch had conducted their colonial rule. Their energies had only too obviously been directed solely to using the wealth of the archipelago to enrich Holland. The pro-independence party in the islands had been permitted minimal influence. Now, with live memories of the total and immediate collapse of Dutch military resistance in 1942 against the Japanese invaders, it was too late to turn the clock back. Observing the nationalists in British India confident with rapid independence soon to be gained, the more educated Indonesians, particularly the Javanese, saw in a socialist commonwealth a future which they were determined should not be frustrated. But there were immediate tasks which demanded a strong military presence. To be sure, there were Dutch troops in Australia, but not on the spot in Indonesia. Thousands of Dutch, including women internees, still languished in camps in the interior, their captors having handed them over to the nationalists. Batavia was an island, or at best with its port, a salient in a hostile surround. The situation warranted the presence of a full corps of British and Indian troops, tense after a British brigadier together with a number of recently released internees had been killed by a mob.

On arrival by flying boat (how scenic and civilized they were as a means of transport!), I was offered lodgings by our military attaché, Colonel Laurens van der Post. Particularly badly treated by the Japanese in his P.O.W.

camp in Java, Van der Post has since acquired the aura of a guru on matters environmental and to do with the Third World generally. He has also become known as a confidant of the Prince of Wales. At that time, he was using his influence with leading Indonesian politicians to try and further some form of stable Indonesian government which might be able to work with the Dutch, presuming immediate independence to be unattainable. Quite often, these talks took place in the house we occupied, a colonial mansion of some solidity. All the same, dinner and politics were occasionally interrupted by tracer bullets rattling across the sky overhead, whereupon guests sensibly dived under the table.

When the Dutch Governor, General van Mook, arrived, great efforts were made to re-establish the past, but it never looked as though it would be possible to do more than hold a perimeter round main centres. The United Nations later sent a distinguished American, Dr. Graham, on a mission of mediation, but nothing much came out of the protracted talks and gradually the more thinking Dutch began to realise that things would never be the same again. The view, many times expressed to me by Dutchmen I had met as P.O.W., that it could take a long time to "bring the natives back to a realisation of their proper attitude," was to prove far truer than they imagined.

Our British official Mission was an old-fashioned Dutch colonial building with a temporary hutment at its side which served as an information cum library office. Here the Consul (Information), a highly talented Scot who had served in SHAEF during the war, and I, as his vice-consular assistant, worked. The British military, who were in effective control for another eighteen months, oversaw a camp nearby which housed several thousand Japanese P.O.W. Two of them, a colonel and a major, were allocated to us. They did odd jobs, ran errands and were generally model characters. When they were eventually repatriated we were pleased to have presented to us with some ceremony a handsome scroll on which, in elaborate characters, it was stated that they had been well and honorably treated. One had told us that he had been an editor on the *Asahi Shimbun,* one of Japan's leading newspapers.

For several years there were in effect two regimes on the island of Java. In 1948, I was asked to go and talk to the Indonesian Minister of Information in the capital of the then Republic at Jocjakarta on the south of the island, an ancient city and most picturesque. I was able to get there by train, and found myself on arrival well nigh the only Westerner there. My business did not take long and, in the evening, I was sitting in my small, old-fashioned hotel when a boy arrived in full Javanese costume with a note: the "Prince" requested my company at dinner the following evening. I accepted and the boy retired. This was not the Sultan, but a member of an ancient Javanese princely line. So come the next evening, a battered taxi arrived and I was driven to the palace. It was a scene reminiscent of Hollywood. Saluted by a majordomo with magnificent headdress and sarong, I was escorted to a low, heavily carved building with a dais where my host would receive me. Flickering fires, fragrant with scented logs, burned in front, and lithe dancers performed gracefully, their hands more like tendrils than limbs. Very soon a young, richly attired personage stepped out from the back of the building to greet me: "My dear fellow," said he in impeccable English, "How very nice of you to come. It's a pleasure to meet someone from Oxford."

My journey took me next day a few miles east, visiting the Borobudur, which was sadly invaded by jungle plants, but enormously impressive with its rows of Buddhas. Apart from the official guide, I had the site to myself. Over to the town of Madiun, where I had an introduction to the local Marxist leader, an old man with a Ho Chi Minh beard who grilled me unmercifully about the iniquities of capitalism. He had heard that the British Labour Government were just as bad as its Conservative Government predecessors had been in resisting the rightful upsurge of the British people. He spoke good Dutch, and it was quite easy to get the drift; less easy perhaps to make any convincing rebuttal. I returned to my lodgings. As I went to bed, however, I noticed two men approaching the building. About three in the morning, talking was going on in not very low tones just outside the door. I realised that they were "on guard" but also that they were not friendly. Indeed one said to the other in Malay, "If we killed this fellow, who is clearly a spy, nobody over there (meaning presumably Jakarta) would know." I did not wait for any further conversation but quickly set a solid Dutch armchair against the door. No more sleep that night! It did not come as a surprise to read in the press back in England some months later that there had been a sizeable communist revolt in the same town, Madiun, which had been put down with heavy loss of life.

William Mortimer Drower

The dreariness of the Indonesian political stalemate, the absence of any goods in the shops after the Japanese occupation and the paucity of civilised entertainment meant that infrequent trips to Singapore were specially welcome. It was pleasant to meet friends in the patrician atmosphere of the dignified old Raffles Hotel, with its gin slings and dinner dances. The shops, too, were well-stocked, goods being obtainable there which were rarely available back in England. All the same, getting round the countryside in Indonesia was remarkably interesting in those pre-package tour days. I once enjoyed a sea trip on an ancient coastal steamer of some hundred and fifty tons which plied between Batavia, the Celebes and Surabaya. The captain was an old Dutchman straight out of Conrad with his glasses of Bols. His account of his father's memories of the 1883 Krakatoa cataclysm was gripping. The latter had been many miles distant from the eruption, which had killed thousands, terrified many times that number and sent enormous waves round the globe. I was surprised to discover that he did not share the "Dutch Club" view of the iniquity of the nationalists and the desirability of immediate return of the old Dutch colonial regime. That was the past, he observed philosophically. Holland knew the area far better than other countries, and her expertise in commercial matters would ensure recuperation.

Air travel was more hand to mouth than nowadays. I wrote my family the following about a flight from Bali to Macassar: "The taxi, ordered for seven, did not arrive. Nor at seven fifteen, nor seven thirty. Frantic calls to the somnolent garage. At seven forty-one, a jalopy arrived on four wheels and the race was on. We drove like hell, I threatening to chuck the fellow out of the taxi unless he broke the speed limit consistently. Past the guard on the drome we lurched and found at the booking office Oriental Impassivity supreme. 'Very sorry. Plane now starting...' It looked as though the clerk was right. The Dakota was whirring like a dragon-fly on a twig and the door was shut. I leaped through the door and ran to the plane, the wheels of which were moving determinedly. Placing myself in its track, I signalled like the heroine in a Wild West train robbery. Earphoned figures high above began to notice that all was not well. The brakes crunched; I bawled, 'Taxi niet gekomen' and head-shakings at first horizontal and then vertical ensued. I scrambled ladderless into the unwilling entrance of the plane and flung in the luggage, most of which landed in the lap of a Chinese woman attired in cretonne and baby. We flew off in a cloudless sky."

It was agreeable to be almost the only visitor then in Bali. True, an Englishman who wrote a gardening column in the *Singapore Times* lived from time to time up on the mountain; a couple of Belgian painters were well established, both with handsome Balinese dancer wives. One or two Dutch military men were there, but that was all. An elderly and sophisticated Balinese prince put me up, and I slept on a kind of dais in a pavilion, open at the sides, with gilded decorations round the elaborately thatched roof. He courteously introduced me to several artists and woodcarvers, several of whose works are now in our house. They, in turn, took me to village "inns"— palm-roofed huts where, late in the evening, there was gamelan music, dancing and much drinking of rice wine. The dancers were mostly very young indeed. We ate sateh — Indonesian shish-kebab with chillies and peanut sauce— and watched the shadow plays which relate the stories of the Ramayana, the triumph of the Monkey god, Hanuman, over the wicked witch. It was a dreamlike experience. One evening, I was taken to the now renowned ketchak monkey dance, which a Dutch ethnologist had shortly before the Japanese invasion helped to revive. Rightly, this astonishing performance is nowadays a regular feature of tourist schedules. On my second visit to that fascinating island, a schooner tied up at the little port near Den Pasar, the capital. She was captained by an enterprising American named Johnson, who had been there often before. He used to contribute travel articles to the *National Geographic* magazine, deriving his crew mainly from well-heeled Ivy League students who were happy to pay for adventure. A meeting in a bar with a Yale man concluded with us arranging to climb Mount Bali together, which towers superbly over the terraced landscape. Porters were arranged, and shortly we set off through the lush paddy fields, with the women, at that time still unencumbered by Playtex uplift, moving gracefully along the paths past the innumerable little shrines, each provided with beautifully woven reed cups filled with rice delicacies. A few days before, one of the Belgian artists who had built himself a house in the hills above Den Pasar had invited me to lunch. Being assiduously attended by his strikingly beautiful and minimally apparelled attendants, one required some determination to keep one's mind on the food!

After this spread, we repaired to the village square. There, on the ground, was set out a large variety of tasty morsels in woven containers, together with cups of rice wine. "Drink up, you demons," the local priest was declaiming. "Take your fill. Hurry up!" And soon after, villagers came round and knocked over the drinks, scattering the rice and the rest of the food. Then they returned with staves and beat the ground hard, all around. This was to make sure that the ground spirits, whose temper was regarded as uncertain, would be driven off. They would be, for a while at least, incapable of mischief now that they were bloated with food and muzzy with strong liquor.

As my American companion and I moved higher up Mount Bali, we could see smoke curling from a crater near the summit. The porters began to chant a curious ditty as they climbed. I asked the rais, or headman, what they were singing about. Embarrassed, he said, "Nothing, Tuan, just a song." But, when pressed, he admitted that they were addressing the Goddess of the Mountain, begging her not to be angry with them, poor men as they were, obliged to earn a few pennies by escorting lunatic foreigners. Several years later, the wrath of the goddess did explode with a vengeance, blowing the top of the mountain completely away and causing casualties estimated at over ten thousand.

Lombok is separated from Bali by a twenty mile strait where the current rushes along. The island suggested a climb, since its highest volcanic peak—Mount Rinjani — rises impressively twelve thousand, two hundred and twenty-five feet above the Pacific. Lombok has features of particular interest to natural scientists. For one thing, its flora and fauna differ from those on Bali and Java to the west; apparently that strait constitutes a sort of natural boundary dividing off Australia. Here my companion was a Dutch lieutenant. Gibbon apes screamed and shouted warnings to each other, swinging frenetically from creeper to creeper, as we made our way up from the coast. The wide variety of birds, both in coloring and song, was astonishing. We camped half way up the mountain, and I remember staring at a moon which looked bigger and more strikingly luminous than ever before in my experience. The last couple of thousand feet were of crunchy soft black ash like Mount Fuji. From the summit, one could look down into a great gash in the volcano at the bottom of which were two crater lakes, one brilliantly violet, testimony to earlier, mighty eruptions.

Back in the capital, which was losing its Dutch name Batavia and assuming that of Jakarta, the clammy heat, the crowds and the general dilapidation were not cheerful. Drinks parties were a refuge for many. The diplomatic round was notable for the French Minister's champagne, and his stunningly attractive lady friend. One of my colleagues, who was cursed with a termagant of a wife, found the chatter at most parties so repetitive and boring that he longed to get out and home, and leaned often on the shoulder of the Scotch bottle. Some people became distinctly odd: one evening, working late, I was urgently summoned by our minister. He was holding a telegram in his hand. "I want you to get this sent off," he said. I read it and could hardly believe my eyes. I knew that my chief had not been out of Jakarta for some days, but here he was describing a conversation just held with President Sukarno, far from Jakarta and most certainly not on the telephone. Spirit communication was taking the place of the normal diplomatic channels. Brashly, I flatly refused to send the telegram.

In later years, I should have found a better expedient, but immature and in the heat of a tropical evening, I reacted in a way which, though it did not result in an official rebuke from Whitehall, cannot greatly have improved my chances of promotion in the Service. The minister was removed to another post and given his retirement pretty soon afterwards. Air-conditioning not having arrived, the constant political tension and oppressive atmosphere of Jakarta were at least escapable. The old Dutch settlement close by, its 16th century Portugese fort and handsome old Protestant church were attractive colonial relics. There were also cooler places an hour or so away in the mountains. Bandung was one, about five thousand feet above the humid coastal plain. Dutch residents used before the 1941 war to drive up there, and many had built holiday bungalows. Sukarno, the Indonesian president, certainly thought it a pleasant area and soon took over the Dutch governor-general's summer palace. A few miles from Bandung on the huge and fertile slope of an extinct volcano, Dutch scientists had established a botanical garden. Since a bungalow nearby, previously occupied by a member of the garden's staff was available for rent, a party of us from the Consulate General decided to spend a weekend there. We duly arrived, accompanied by the military attaché who brought with him his Indian bearer. In all we were about eight persons including two wives and one baby in arms. There was still in progress a guerilla war between the Dutch and the nationalist Indonesians which was not to come to an end until, with Washington applying both stick and Marshall Aid carrot, independence was finally granted in 1949. The Dutch Army had carried out several "police operations" to clear out armed bands and widen the perimeter near the European occupied towns. The religion of Java is Muslim, not as a rule in a strict form, but fundamentalist groups have often been a truculent element, especially when vigorous "anti-colonialist" passions have run high. The Band of Allah—Hizb Allah—though small, provided a militant voice among the activists.

As a precaution, our military colleague had seen to it that each man in the party should carry some form of weapon against a possible emergency, though this seemed a little extravagant. We arrived before noon in glorious weather and enjoyed the delicious breath of the cool mountain breeze. The swimming pool had been filled by the Dutch caretaker, and we were not slow to plunge in. Sitting beside it, after lunch, I remember putting on my portable phonograph a fine, new recording of Schubert's great "Ninth Symphony." The third movement had been reached before someone looked down the long road up from the valley and said, "There's a procession coming up." But very soon after that we heard the crackle of rifle shots. Flags, unmistakably violent red, were waving. We "got the message" and retired to the bungalow with some speed. In front of its low surrounding wall, the caretaker had some time before dug a slit trench of sorts. The women lay flat inside the bungalow, and we prepared for a siege, equipped with our very modest armament. Ten rounds of ammunition were all that accompanied my .38 inch bore revolver. Even the light machine-gun which our military companion had decided to bring was not provided with any generous reserve of ammunition. The "procession" came up to within a couple of hundred yards and opened fire in a vigorous demonstration of hostile intent, made clearer by the brandishing of flashing krises (Malay cutlasses) and cries of "Akan Potong Belanda!" which meant that as presumed Dutch settlers we were to be carved up. (What a bore, one felt, after seven years of war!) We replied with fire, though the military attaché found that his bearer was shaking with fear so badly that he decided to use him as a sandbag to kneel on in order to assist his aim.

Almost at once we saw one assailant fall and another screamed as though badly wounded. Whereupon they retreated but then, a little later, another worrying tactic was employed—that of attempting to take us in the rear. We were astonished and delighted to hear a loud explosion followed by diminishing yells from the back of the building. We found out that the caretaker had kept in prudent reserve for a similar emergency a grenade which he had just lobbed at his adversaries with considerable effect. They did not repeat the manoeuvre. Then, there was a very long pause. Night falls early in the tropics, and we guessed that should the band attack us then, using as cover the surrounding trees, our chances of survival were not good. Near five o'clock we could hear a whirring sound up the mountain, distinctly the engine of a motorcycle. Shots followed. The motorcycle seemed to stop and then restart, the noise of the exhaust fading into the distance. About an hour later, when night was ominously near and sniping had started again with our ammunition practically spent, we heard the roar of heavy vehicles. Hurrah! these were armoured Dutch troop carriers. It seemed that an alert dispatch rider down in the valley had heard the sound of shooting and had decided to investigate. Fired upon, he had retired to report the matter to company headquarters a mile or so away. Our rescuers were soon with us, wrapped women and baby in blankets and took us down to hot drinks and sandwiches, before seeing us home in cars back to Jakarta. Meantime, the Dutch unit settled down to defend the bungalow against any further assault which, in fact, came that night but was repulsed with more casualties, we were later told.

My tour of duty over, return to the U.K. was by a form of transport now sadly unavailable. The Danish East Asiatic Company still ran a five thousand ton vessel on a service which took in Singapore, Penang, Colombo, the Suez Canal, Genoa and Glasgow over about seven weeks. In company with about one dozen other passengers, this was a delightful way of returning gently to the comparative rigors of a European winter. Florence in winter can be dreadfully cold, with the wind sweeping down from the Alps. The ship's doctor and I both felt, though, that we had started a love affair with that wonderful city and with the Italian language which owes so very much to its influence. Italy is still ravishly charming, whatever agonies it suffers from the Mafia and ingrained corruption.

CHAPTER NINE

EGYPT AFTER FAROUK

By early 1949 I was back in London where I spent a year or so before finding myself back in Cairo, posted to our Embassy. The unlovely King Farouk had a few months before being deposed and was to fritter away his few remaining years with bimbos in Europe. Supernationalist young officers had made a successful coup, and General Naguib was now at the head of the new Egyptian government, already striving to throw away the remaining features of the old condominium. Cairo was nothing like the size it is today, and the appalling overcrowding of many quarters of the city which is now so shocking to health workers had not yet been aggravated by thousands upon thousands of peasants streaming into the capital. Nor had foreign tourism, developed to the point where it has in the last three decades, formed a crucial element in Egypt's economy.

Beginning my posting with an ill-judged stay on a floating hotel on the Nile, resulting in a bout of typhoid, I found very kindly accommodation in a boarding type establishment run by an aged Scots lady who had been in

Egypt for many years. Tension between the new Egyptian regime and us British, who still kept troops in the capital, was growing. Negotiations with the nationalists to include an agreement on the future of the Suez Canal had already begun, and they continued in a desultory fashion until Gamal Abdul Nasser's 1954 seizure of power. Churchill never made any talks with Egypt easier by insisting on points which were hard for the Egyptians to accept. Doubtless to him, the "loss of Egypt" was something as indigestible as the independence of India had been.

For recreation I took up the flute, an instrument eminently portable, soon finding a teacher and friend in a musicologist named Hans Hellman. It was he who had been largely responsible for "bringing to life" the golden trumpets found in the tomb of Tutankhamen. Verdi, writing the score of "Aida," set the tone range of the trumpets, which play such an important part in the opera, a good deal higher than was usual, and received criticism for so doing. Hellman was able to show, after careful restoration of the centuries-long squashed instruments, that Verdi had it just right. Their tone was indeed strident and high in pitch. Apropos of Verdi it was most evocative of the 19th century to hear "Aida" played in the old wooden Cairo opera house where it had been originally performed at the time of the opening of the Suez Canal. Sadly, either by accident or design, the opera house was burned to the ground within a few years.

Our Cairo Embassy was on a fine site overlooking the Nile. Much perfunctory diplomatic hospitality, some of which inevitably tedious, was to be expected. To enliven matters one lighthearted junior military attaché at a buffet reception one evening spied a very large Egyptian Army

Major, who evidently believing himself unobserved, pick up a dressed cold chicken from the sideboard and tuck it into his tunic pocket. Our bright young spark quickly sidled up, took a bottle of mayonnaise and emptied it into the outraged major's pocket, observing, "You must have some mayonnaise with your chicken, my dear chap!" It is unlikely that British-Egyptian relations made any great stride forward that day.

Soon I was joined by my recently widowed mother. She already knew Cairo pretty well from her travels as a journalist early in the century. The bustling bazaars and the mosques she found as little changed as the pyramids close by. One thing depressed her: the reports from scholars of the regular thefts of treasures from the great Cairo museum, ill-paid and venal attendants probably mostly to blame. Over the years, several European ladies had established a tradition of being knowledgeable about the many mosques and tombs dotted about in the city and of being on the necessary good terms with the imams. We got to know a Mrs. Devonshire, who was French. She had published *Rambles in Cairo* which is still looked on as a classic. On most Sunday afternoons, she took parties round the old city, spicing the tour with fascinating historical and architectural comments. Since that particularly interesting area of old Cairo, the City of the Dead, a confusion of stone tombs, is now crowded by indigent peasants, that part of the tour today would have to be omitted.

Wishing, less improvingly, to play golf, I joined the Gezirah Club, which was about to modify its policy of excluding all but a few Egyptians. (Very soon it would be taken over by the Egyptian Army.) Possessed of good tennis and swimming facilities, it was still run by a traditional British committee retaining rigidly unprogressive ideas. At one point in the Second World War, when officers were seeking in Cairo rest and recreation from Rommel, a senior member of the club committee was said to have sallied forth at midnight upon the course and to have discovered on the welcoming softness of one of the sandbunkers, an officer and his girlfriend in *medias res*. "I say!" he is said to have spluttered, "You can't do that here, you know! Why, you aren't even members!" The third golf fairway ran the length of a private road where the excellent American hospital and a row of mansions were to be found, including one belonging to Princess Fawzia, sister to the Shah of Iran, which had a number of chimneys. It was only too easy for golfers to "pull" their balls out of bounds. When the house was surveyed a few years later - a vast number of golf balls was found in and around the chimneys, having been used by the screaming kites, who circled tirelessly over the players, as surrogate eggs.

We had a joint Army and Foreign Office outpost in the Canal Zone where British troops were concentrated, as they had been since the war of 1939-45, to protect the Canal. I spent some part of my Egyptian posting there, looking out upon the Great Bitter Lake. There it was that I met my wife Constance on a tennis-court, she being accurately introduced as a far better performer than myself. Her chuckle impressed and delighted me even more than her court strokes. After little more than a week, I proposed, to be rejected, but perseverance paid off in the end. She comes from a family with long connections with the sea: both her father and brother have been pilots at the port of Liverpool. During the Second World War, she joined the WRENS (Women's Royal Naval Service), won her commission and then worked in naval operations before being posted to Australia, where Prince Philip was to be eyed by numerous designing hostesses. As a matter of wry coincidence I was "down under" in 1947 on a visit to my wartime comrades and might easily have met her there. After the war she had taken a job with the War Office and that is how our paths crossed in the Middle East.

Before we finished our tours, Nasser had pushed Neguib out and taken charge flamboyantly. The Suez fiasco, which strained Anglo-American relations so badly for a while, was shortly to occur. But even Nasser, courted sedulously by the Soviet Union, was soon to be worried by the rapid growth of Muslim fundamentalism which threatened his regime. With imams "working" the mosques, the Muslim Brotherhood was already gaining recruits to its anti-Western fundamentalism. This movement, then not thirty years old, nurtured in the dusty jostling streets of Cairo, rapidly spread to other Arab countries and still rattles their rulers. More recently, calls for Jihad—holy war against the infidel—have been proclaimed by both the Ayatollah Khomeini and Saddam Hussein as a sure-fire expedient to gain popular support. But, in fact, Jihad is contained in the Koran as a constant injunction laid on the Muslim faithful sedulously to spread the True Faith, and is not as many imagine solely a rallying cry in battle. In much of Iraq, as most recent events have shown, the adherents of the Shiah sect, who look back with intense nostalgia to the murder of Muhammad's son-in-law and likely successor Ali, have long felt unprivileged and defensive.

Egypt After Farouk

The intolerance and backward-turning fanaticism of fundamentalist Islam has stood in sharp relief against the Egyptian government's steady toleration of Copts, members of an ancient Christian sect which over the years has provided many notable Egyptian public servants, including Mr. Butros-Ghali. A favourite expedition by diplomats was by car to the second century Coptic monastery in the desert not far from Alexandria. Jews were numerous in the European communities of Cairo and Alexandria. Their synagogue in Cairo was notable as a charming building, which I hope still survives. It was not until several years later that Jews suffered real discrimination.

Beside the gleaming minarets of the great mosque of Khadimein in Baghdad, an event takes place every year in Muharram, the first month of the Moslem year, when Shiah male believers, stripped to the waist, rhythmically flog themselves with chains, crying out "Ali!"— bewailing his murder—as they trudge feverishly along the street. Blood flows liberally. Keen to see this while I was in Baghdad in early 1946 and having asked a Muslim friend of my father's whether be thought it feasible, he replied, "Yes, but only provided I equip you with Arab disguise. Come about five in the morning to such and such an address and you will be able to see the procession from an upstairs window." This was done, and it was an eerie experience. The chief surgeon at the hospital was a Scot, friendly with my parents, and he told them that the rapidity with which the wounds healed on the backs of those believers who were afterwards brought in for treatment was remarkable and barely explicable.

Without the air conditioning which is now general, summer leave from Cairo heat was most welcome. All the same, I shall always regret that instead of then taking a river boat or train up the Nile, I missed many of the great Pharaonic temples with their marvelously preserved wall paintings. Instead, I flew to meet a girl friend in Venice. Unique and perpetually enticing, that wicked old city was still relatively unencumbered by hordes of tourists, and much easier to enjoy than today. The hamlet which is nearest to us in Somerset remembers a lively character of the early 17th century, one Tom Coryate, who, becoming bored with life at home with his father—the parish priest — decided to walk to Venice. This he actually did and published a most amusing account of his various adventures en route. Unlikely to beat the bandits of the Alps, he joined them (for the time being). On return, he was a hero both in his community and at Court, and his shoes long dangled in the village church.

My sister Peggy's interest in Ancient Egypt has been professional and intensely satisfying, first as an excavator and later lecturing to parties of visitors to Egypt, year after year, up the Nile. Her first mentor was a remarkable man, Professor Flinders Petrie, under whom she studied at London University. He was a pioneer in the development of archaeological techniques, stressing in particular the importance of examining and recording fragments of pottery and other objects which earlier scholars had tended to throw away as of little interest. Though, of course, the major finds in the great pyramid area thrilled the world —glistening gold sarcophagi, chariots and so forth—cumulative studies of small finds have made it possible, for instance, to trace the extent of trade contacts between Egypt and the Mediterranean world in the age before

Egypt After Farouk

Homer. Peggy's recent biography of Petrie is the definitive work on this remarkable man.

Despite the bubbling nationalist unrest in Egypt and the emergence of Israel, other parts of the Middle East had so far been spared conflict, destruction or absolute ethnic division. Beirut was exceptionally prosperous and looked upon as the major commercial center east of Suez. On a visit there, I bought Constance, my fiancée, a bangle from one of no less than twenty-three goldsmiths' shops standing in a row. But then, as now, the trappings of Western civilisation hung over a very old, primitive oriental past. Hearing screams from my hotel balcony one evening, I looked down into a traditional Arab garden to see a boy beating a girl unmercifully with a stick. Her cries were loud and pathetic. Perhaps it was only his sister.

Cyprus was very different then too, for both Greek and Turk lived together, as they had done for centuries, in reasonable harmony under a modest British military presence based on NATO. Nicosia, the capital, was also the commercial center with Turks in considerable numbers there. Constance and I were browsing round the shops one day when our eyes lighted on some attractive lapis lazuli colored beads. We went to ask their price. The Turkish shopkeeper looked puzzled. "What do you want them for?" he asked. The reply, "For this lady," provoked peals of laughter. "You must know," he explained, "we put them round the necks of donkeys to keep off the Evil Eye!"

CHAPTER TEN

SWISS ROLE

It was as well that I had not left the United Kingdom in 1941 married. My wife might well have suffered like so many wives and sweethearts the agonies of uncertainty, fear and anxiety, since the Japanese did not observe the conventions in respect of P.O.W., in particular, regarding letters and parcels, Red Cross or personal. There were, one heard after release, many sad cases of marriages simply disintegrating for lack of contact over years. One incident comes to mind of a really bizarre character: it took place in a P.O.W. hut in Thailand about 1943. Loud angry shouting and altercation was heard. So I went along to see what was amiss. The last thing we wanted was for Japanese guards to intervene in any dispute among the men, since they would probably beat them up or place a new restriction on the hut. Very soon the facts came out: the men had been boasting of their female conquests. One Don Juan was expatiating upon the qualities of a young temptress called Millie. Where did she live, another had asked? In so-and-so was the reply. As the reader might now have guessed, the Millie so extolled turned out to be the spouse of the other man. They had come to blows and nastier threats. What happened eventually after the war I do not know. Possibly things were arranged amicably, or simply forgotten.

By 1955, Constance and I were back again in London. We got married and in the spring of 1957, our daughter Sarah was born. We had bought a house high on the Surrey downs some fifteen miles south of St. Paul's Cathedral, whose dome, in those days of frequent fog, quite often protruded above a dirty white blanket. Indeed, after a particularly lethal fog which produced many fatal casualties the government decided that enough was enough and smoke emission regulations were brought in. The effect was both remarkable and immediate. But since then automobile-created smog has undone much of the benefit.

The News Department in the Foreign Office, where I spent some months, has always been seen as important, if only as a training ground for British diplomatists in public relations. It offered excellent chances of meeting interesting people, foreign correspondents, home commentators and academic specialists. Inevitably, some journalists, not usually the most able, looked upon the department as a tiresome obstacle to their stories, a subtle source of distraction and calculated favoritism and disinformation. But, on the whole, our relations with the media were excellent in my time, and friendships transatlantic and continental were made, several of which proved long-lasting.

The Office was far less of a ground for discussion "in depth" than restaurants or a club — the latter a much more agreeable milieu to discuss the Great Leap Forward in China, the rehabilitation of Japan or developments in Indonesia. (Viet Nam was mercifully not yet upon us.) My own club was down Pall Mall, not too far from the pelicans and other soot-flaked birds which squawked and clucked on the lake behind the F.O.'s mock Florentine facade. Club life was already under novel pressure in those days of the Fifties: women were clamouring to be admitted, and as full members, not merely tolerated as occasional guests. Simultaneously club membership was suffering from increasing demands from wives that their menfolk should be back at home in the evening and not, Trollope-like, dawdling late in the club at cards or billiards.

Our university club membership provisions, dating back to the early 19th century, were both vague and gentlemanly, hardly ever requiring invocation. But one fine day crisis struck. One old member had been growing noticeably odd. We had become pretty used to his mumbling about in corners and to his heroic but noisy insistence that he must be allowed to settle his meal bill — "But you've already paid, Sir!" from the cashier. Then several members reported to the shocked club secretary that they had been pounced upon by Mr. X as they put on their overcoats by the club entrance. "Aha! I've caught you! No doubt you saw me coming and have very properly replaced in my coat pocket what you were attempting to remove!"

This was considered too much, or as people might now say— "over the top." Forced resignation was reluctantly proposed if courtesy failed to produce the right result. Alas, close examination of the rules revealed no provision for expulsion if the offending member refused to resign. So in the end a special meeting of the club committee was unwillingly convened at which an appropriate new rule was agreed. Mr. X was summoned and told his fate, whereupon he steadfastly maintained that he was being shamefully traduced.

A chance to go to Geneva as spokesman was too interesting to miss and, in 1959, I joined our delegation to the Conference on the Discontinuance of Nuclear Tests. Our leader of delegation was David Ormsby-Gore, later Lord Harlech, scion of a family which had offered statesmen to the Crown since the days of Queen Elizabeth I. The key figure on the United States side was Glenn Seaborg, heading the U.S. Atomic Energy Commission, who did not appear at the actual conference table. The chief Soviet Delegate was named Tsarapkin, whose name could be translated as the One Who Scratches. (Naturally the Western delegates referred to him as "Old Scratchy.") It was hard going. Stone-walling steadily, the Soviets resisted our every effort to get them to agree to even a very few on-site inspections to detect Russian nuclear explosions. Khruschev, however, must at one point have been persuaded, one year before his fall, that the latest techniques of aerial reconnaissance, together with more sensitive seismic instrumentation, made it counter-productive internationally to go on stalling on at least a ban on air tests. So the 1963 Treaty to that effect was signed in Moscow.

Geneva was the site of other international conferences where the major powers faced each other. One was the conference on Laos, designed to check and delay a further deterioration of the situation in Indo-China. The attempt was not to succeed, and already there was an atmosphere of foreboding in relation to Viet Nam. The difference between the attitude of the delegates from North and South Vietnam was quite striking: the former arrogantly confident, even truculent, the latter restrained and suave. Averell Harriman was the chief U.S. delegate, and it was at that time that he was enabled in Geneva to hold secret probing conversations with the Chinese Foreign Minister, since the Peoples' Republic took an interest in that conference.

Another marathon East-West confrontation was the Eighteen Power General and Complete Disarmament Conference—seventeen nations in reality, as there was always an empty chair left for the French, then under the domination of General de Gaulle. Among the Iron Curtain countries in the conference room was Romania. One day, I received an invitation to dinner with their delegation to be held at a lakeside restaurant, which I knew to be very good. I accepted and duly turned up in the brilliant light of a June full moon. Dinner proceeded together with mundane diplomatic chitchat until the coffee and liqueurs. Then the most senior of the Romanians took me aside and told me that things "had changed" with the advent of Ceauscescu. No longer would Romania be a football of the Soviet Union. We should watch carefully not what the Romanians said, but rather what they did. This interesting change of heart, if not of policy, we reported to London and shortly after we heard that there had been a similar demarche in Warsaw. In the event, that boast of very limited independence was seen to be not entirely without substance. Though the Romanian regime became steadily more and more unpleasant and dictatorial, Soviet leaders found it less easy to count on its automatic servility in all matters.

Another body which used Geneva as its headquarters was the International Parliamentary Union, whose organiser was a former Swiss diplomat, Monsieur de Blonay. Members of various elected national assemblies, including the Westminster Parliament and the Congress of the United States, met in various locations and discussed world problems. With the increase in the number of nations represented in New York, de Blonay hoped to see the I.P.U. recognised as some form of agency of the U.N. This ambition did not meet with favour from any major power so far as I know. Nevertheless, the I.P.U. has provided a useful venue for the exchange of views among politicians, free from local electoral pressures. Our M.P.s used to request the Foreign Office for someone to come along to such meetings to brief them on specific points of policy. It was in this capacity and at such a gathering in Lausanne, that in the spring of 1962, I first became acquainted with members of Congress. Notably effective participants were congressmen Emilio Daddario of Connecticut, Barber Conable of New York, later to head the World Bank, the conservative Ross Adair of Indiana and Bradford Morse of Massachusetts, who became an assistant secretary general at the U.N. On the Senate side, young Senator Frank Church of Idaho, Mike Monroney of Oklahoma and Hugh Scott from Pennsylvania were regulars. One year, Belgrade was the site of the conference, President Tito presiding and showing off his new palace.

A terrible earthquake had just occurred in southern Yugoslavia in the Kossovo area. At that time, rumblings of ethnic divisions in Yugoslavia were heard very clearly by the Western Powers, and there were actual riots involving people of Albanian stock. One delegate to the I.P.U. meeting was the ineffable Madame Nhu from Saigon who caused a considerable stir with her jewels and reputation. I found myself in later years at other I.P.U. conferences — 1964 in Copenhagen and 1965 in Ottawa.

Planning vacations when conferences are proceeding is no easy matter, yet our little family was able to see much of Europe, for we were centrally poised in Switzerland. For most of our stay in Geneva, we inhabited one half of an old house which was on the site of a farm owned by the brother of John Calvin, that stern 16th century religious dictator. The main staircase, with its elaborate iron balustrade, was neatly divided in two, the other half of the house being lived in by a Swiss architect and his family. The garden was large and set out in old French style with all manner of pergolas and vegetables and flowerbeds. It was also equipped with a venerable gardener with whiskers in an "O." Our daughter loved him dearly. Chattering French with the architect's children, she went for a couple of years to the local primary school, where the atmosphere was quite old-world as were her teachers.

Voltaire's house at Ferney was just two miles distant over the French frontier, reached by a small road which had been, until the middle of the 19th century, marked by a gallows. There was still a slight element of criminality about, since meat and butter were smuggled in regularly as far less expensive, impost free. Across from us was a

Swiss Role

Rothschild estate which boasted a private zoo. Our British Mission, which has since been given back to the original owners, was an 18th century mansion enjoying a magnificent view over the Lake of Geneva, with its huge sprouting fountain and Mont Blanc crowning the alpine panorama in the background. Sightseeing in Switzerland itself was delightful and possible on many weekends. We did not ski, since it seemed that starting this perilous sport at over forty was not a good idea, only too easily a broken leg or worse—a self-inflicted wound and a bore to one's working colleagues.

On the subject of absences, it was abundantly gossiped that the aristocratic leader of the Italian Delegation at the Disarmament talks had a girl friend not so many miles away at a delightful spot on the edge of the Lake of Geneva. An extra session of the conference was suddenly called one hot afternoon, but no Italian appeared. "Oho!" chuckled the Soviet delegate, who had a sense of humor; "Evidently the distinguished delegate has very much better things to do!" In fact socially the Swiss seem difficult to know well. They naturally regard the transient goings on at the Palace of Nations in Geneva as hardly likely to engage long-term friendships, and tend to keep to themselves.

Lord Harlech, a fine man to work for, asked me before he set out for Washington to take up the position of ambassador—where he would be daily in touch with his friend, President Kennedy, whether I would like to serve in the United States. And so in October, 1964, the Drowers found themselves on the grand old "Queen Mary," ploughing through half a hurricane. It must have been one of the old lady's very last crossings. New York looked superb, just as in many a good film. We found a friendly taxi and struggled with our baggage to the railroad station. Thus began a fascinating ten years the other side of the Atlantic.

CHAPTER ELEVEN

A CAPITOL FELLOW

The job initially assigned to me when we had settled into Washington life, having found a pleasant house just off the Glover Archbold Park, was a general public relations brief. This I soon found unsatisfactory. Thirty years ago, as now, the cream of the Washington media expected to talk only with ambassadors and ministers of foreign missions, not with spokespersons, save on questions of detail. In London, they tend today to be surprised and often irritated at not being granted direct and immediate access to government departments. Early in 1965, however, Alan McCall-Judson who had been our congressional liaison anchorman for a number of years, retired, and I was offered the assignment. Thanks to him and his forerunners as well as to various Interparliamentary Union contacts, I enjoyed a good start.

Certainly Lord Harlech, our ambassador, who was soon to be called back to the U.K., had made many friendships in Washington including on Capitol Hill. Sir Patrick Dean and his successors John Freeman and Lord

A Capitol Fellow

Cromer were to give me the backing I needed. They well understood what had not, frankly, been taken in for a long time by some politicians and bureaucrats in London—that by the provisions of the American Constitution, decisions are made by the Congress as much as by the President and his administration. Thus, it was simply not enough to say: "The Americans accept this."

It had been in our darkest days of the Second World War that Sir Isaiah Berlin, now a venerated professor of the international politico-philosophical hierarchy, had come to Washington and had set out to ascertain the temper of the Congress, the variety of views held by legislators of importance, the degree to which they might be prepared to listen to the British point of view and, if possible, look more kindly than they would otherwise have done on British wartime initiatives. He was to make no bones about the nature of his assignment and, in the series of despatches home which have recently been published, he has commented that his contacts on and off the Hill alike were perfectly aware of what he was doing. He was something new—an official British lobbyist—a diplomatic political animal, and an eminently successful one. Together with Archie Campbell, a rollicking and almost legendary Embassy press officer who operated around the Press Club on 14th Street, Isaiah Berlin greatly helped to transform the outlook of many leading Americans toward Britain in her struggle over in Europe. Even more importantly, he provided much more accurate assessments for Whitehall of the proposals, reservations and sometimes prejudices to be found among members of the Congress and Administration. This was achieved at a time when we had most need, when our chances of coming through against the brutal power of the two major Axis Powers were, by any historical standard, slim. Again, when the Second World War was at an end and Americans were tempted to wonder whether they had not been too indulgent, and when too many British politicians persisted in unrealistic assumptions about how much clout the British Empire still possessed, Berlin's type of reporting was crucial.

"The American desk" was thus established. There had been a kind of succession, and I was now simply the latest occupant of the slot. Clearly Alan had made many friends in both parties and he took me to meet them. Hale Boggs of Louisiana and Dick Bolling of Missouri, both key figures in the House of Representatives (to mention but two), merited early calls. The Wednesday Club, with its group of liberal Republican legislators such as Barber Conable of New York, later at the helm of the World Bank, were welcoming. Bradford Morse early counselled me to keep a sharp eye on "Tip" O'Neill; there, he explained, was a man whose judgement was a touchstone. He would not probably have known then that he was talking of a future Speaker.

It would be fair to say that Middle Western Republicans looked coolly, to say the least, on the 1964 Labour Government of Harold Wilson. To some of them, a nation being subjected to declaredly socialist reforms, which had just produced the Beatles, was not likely to be a reliable ally against the multiple wiles of the Kremlin. Nor did the revelations of the Burgess and Maclean spy scandals diminish suspicions about Britain's reliability in intelligence matters. With the Cuba fiasco not far back in history, the concept of the Evil Empire seemed to an incoming Britisher very real in many parts of the U.S.A. well before Reagan. So, quite apart from Viet Nam, I found a degree of caution at first among the more conservative members of the Grand Old Party. Having said that I have little doubt, though, that several conservatives I had met with the Interparliamentary Union passed on a kindly word when asked for a personal "run-down." Generally, I was courteously received and generously treated. For their part, the Democrats, Southern and Northern, were enormously obliging.

Of course there were ups and downs clearly visible and abundantly reported in relations between the United States and its allies, including Britain, and these especially concerned the Viet Nam war. General de Gaulle was not likely to increase his popularity in a nation of which he had been consistently contemptuous. Such tensions were immediately and obviously reflected in the attitudes of members of the Congress to European diplomats. Although the Australians took part in the war in a very limited way, and although one or two British experts were placed at the disposal of General Ridgeway and subsequent U.S. commanders, there was never a real likelihood that the U.K. would send fighting contingents out to Indochina. Senator Fulbright, who will long be remembered for his scholarship scheme, tended, as chairman of the Senate Foreign Relations Committee, to be scathing in private about the client role, as he saw it, of the U.K. and its acceptance administrations. Also pressures for protective tariffs by the extremely well-financed U.S. commercial lobbies were constantly to be reckoned with, particularly in the course of hearings in the House Committee on Ways and Means. In the matter of commercial aviation the abandonment of the American supersonic aircraft early in the 1970s was accompanied by Commerce Committee asseverations to me and my colleagues at the Embassy that the Concorde aircraft, if it could fly safely, would never, on account of its limited passenger accommodation, be a paying proposition. (To be sure, the full costs of research and development after more than twenty successful years have not yet been met!)

On the other hand during my time in Washington the most influential members of Congress were generally aware of and did not oppose the remarkably close relations which continued, several decades after the Second World War, to inform the intelligence communities of Britain and the U.S. No doubt our liaison with the F.B.I. must have been to some extent vitiated by the slanted reports of Edgar Hoover, especially on the progress of Civil Rights, to which history has now clearly shown him to be hostile. However as an effective counterbalance to that inspired prejudice, Britain, the recent recipient of several million immigrants from non-white populations, largely moved by conscience, was bound to watch what was happening throughout the United States. Partly through the discussions in the Congress Whitehall learned much from the successes and shortcomings of the Great Society programme of Lyndon Johnson and itself brought into being a British commission on racial equality which was later to lead to the creation of a structure to improve and monitor equality between the sexes.

A Capitol Fellow

One attitude pretty widespread on Capitol Hill was an impatience that those squabbling Europeans could not "get their act together." A united Europe was not seen as a menace to the United States, rather as a desirable entity from the defence and commercial points of view — the Cold War was raging and fears of Japanese domination of the markets were beginning to increase. But Northern Ireland with its fossilized historical prejudices was and still continues to be an awkward subject for a Britisher in a country where those of Irish ancestry, real or imagined, were so numerous in politics at every level. "What are you now doing to my people?" hurled one New York senator, I remember. In fact, despite electoral temptations it was surprising that rather few members of the Congress made a leading issue out of Ulster. Facts were something several did not wish to be confused by, especially the ratio of two Protestants to one Catholic in the province. Quite often it seemed that a congressman would take on a member of staff with recognisably "green" credentials, the environmental Greens having hardly yet appeared. So material highly critical of Britain's role in peacekeeping between the two Irish communities would be constantly available, though infrequently used on the floor. Undoubtedly today the situation in Ulster has become more obdurate and polarized—far worse than it was in the Sixties and early Seventies.

If a historian were to be asked to choose ten years of lapidary legislative importance in the history of the United States, I expect that he or she would be likely to consider, if not to select, 1964-74, those years when Constance and I were in Washington. The old Southern Democrat caucus was greatly transformed; equally Republicans found in the South a great number of actual or potential voters of whom they never would have dreamed in the days of President Kennedy. The struggle to reform the House Rules Committee and the part played in this by Congressman Dick Bolling, the Speaker who never was, was a miniature of the battle between the old Southern Democratic traditions and newer, radical ideas.

Similarly the creation of the Democratic Study Group by a team of intelligent, very hard-working reform-minded congressmen meant that the president's Great Society strategists could count upon its steady support in that great series of measures designed to transform the country. Later there was to be an internal struggle for control of the group, but such conflicts are beguiling to an observer who must keep his or her eye on the actual issues. There was certainly a desire in those years to tighten up the personal conduct of members, and the creation of the Committees on Ethics and Standards was a result. The widely publicised cases of a committee chairman like Adam Clayton Powell or, less flagrantly that of Senator Thomas Dodd, were clearly unacceptable to a body of legislators who wished to get away from the old concept of wheeling and dealing in whiskey-drenched, smoke-filled rooms. To a Britisher, there is always too much money about in Washington, and the temptations of jobbery must be enormous. I knew well the immensely talented and witty man, Representative Frank Thompson, Democrat of New Jersey, who unfortunately fell foul of the tightened law on campaign funding. He usually had ready in the evening a snippet of gossip, a funny story and a glass of Scotch. A quite different close friend was Representative Charles (Chuck) Mosher, Republican of Oberlin, Ohio. Scholar, man of sunny and stimulating personality, he was to be signally honoured on his retirement from the House by the Committee on Science and Technology when they selected him as their chief of staff when he was past seventy years old.

Mosher was one of the stalwarts of the Wednesday Club of liberal-minded Republicans who were frequently to be found in the gymnasium of the Capitol. One of them was Frank Horton of Rochester, New York, who told friends that he had once had to make the choice between running for Congress and becoming a professional baseball player with the New York Yankees. He kept up with his old baseball stars, and my wife and I were able on more than one occasion to meet some of them in splendid seats at the Washington Stadium. Another Wednesday character was Chuck Whalen, otherwise Charles Whalen Jr. of Dayton, Ohio, who was always helpful with sound middle of the road advice on how things were likely to develop. The Marching and Chowder Republicans took a little more knowing.

Some part of the time of a diplomat is inevitably and frequently unprofitably taken up with visitors, from the Parliament or otherwise, wanting to get a picture of what is going on. Most are content to obtain an impression of the general legislative sequence, which they may fortify with visits to the galleries of the Chambers. Others have appointments and business to discharge with individual members and their staffs. Often I went along with them. As might be expected, in the Embassy Chancery—then a team of about thirty—there were specialists on defence and defence procurement, finance including the International Monetary Fund, attachés for civil air and labor matters and so forth. Each would maintain good relations with staff on the Hill as with the relevant department of the Administration. It was up to me to offer some background help, assess possible congressional attitudes, advise them who might be a good person on the Hill to approach. As mentioned the Committee of Ways and Means hearings dealing with trade bills must always be of high interest, and we most often had someone in the committee room listening as well as studying the published record. The senior staff members of committees in both Houses were nearly always excellent to deal with. Carl Marcy of the Senate Foreign Relations Committee I remember as one particularly able professional who nearly always seemed to be able to find time to talk.

Apropos it was to a Britisher curious that the House Foreign Affairs Committee had so little clout in matters of foreign policy since it was apparently concerned almost exclusively with the subject of foreign aid. There were few votes in foreign aid. However the NATO subcommittee was of considerable importance and its chairman, Congressman Wayne Hays, whose staff included young women who appeared to have little experience of typewriting, was a man of importance in that context.

Not all visitors from the U.K. were political. One day, I was asked by a very well-known English portrait painter whether I might suggest some possible sitters for portraits. The request seemed immediately to point to the person of the then Vice-President, Mr. Spiro Agnew. Be sure to make him look like a Roman Senator, I advised. The artist approached Mr. Agnew and a lucrative commission was rapidly agreed. In due course the portrait was displayed with some panache at a party in Georgetown. There indeed was a fine Roman figure, the head discreetly illumined—the noble glance of a Lycurgus. The V.P. was said to be very pleased, and later we heard that the Maryland Statehouse had caused it to be hung in a special place of honour near the entrance. But disastrous events were to ensue. The V.P. retired very suddenly from the scene, and the Maryland legislature proceeded firmly but discreetly to remove the portrait from the ceremonious prominence originally accorded and secreted it, it was alleged, down in the basement.

Washington is excusably looked upon as the city of the lobbyist. In Westminster, by contrast, special interest lobbying was hardly admitted to exist before the Second World War. More recently, in particular as a consequence of the privatisation of utilities and straight commercial pressures both inside the GATT and the Common Market, there has been far greater frankness about the extent and variety of lobbying activity throughout Britain. Members of Parliament these days are obliged, somewhat grudgingly, to register their extraparliamentary financial interests. No inhibitions about admitting to be a lobbyist in Washington! Special interest lobbyists were both numerous and fully declared, professional to a degree and exceptionally well-informed. Since I was a lobbyist of sorts for Her Majesty's Government, it behove me to pay careful attention to the recognised top practitioners. The National Rifle Association fell somewhat outside my brief! One of them was former Congressman Andrew J. Biemiller of the A.F.L./C.I.O. who for years ran a most effective team. He knew everybody, was most "clubable" as Samuel Johnson would have said, and furthermore lived in the same street in Bethesda as my wife and myself. (His roses were superb.) Through him, I got to know a number both of members and of labor union personalities and was offered some understanding of how a lobbyist approaches his "targets," making himself helpful with up-to-date information when needed and, in Biemiller's case at least, even suggesting wording of possible legislation. As to single issue lobbies, these were just coming in. Ralph Nader approached the environment with missionary purpose. The so-called pro-life lobby had hardly begun to seek to impose its will.

Lobbyists operating on the Hill were and doubtless still are lavish providers of goodies in the form of lecture assignments or campaign contributions. Obviously I had little or nothing to sell. Perhaps an invitation to lunch, or perhaps to a relaxed dinner with the ambassador in his baroque Lutyens residence at 3100 Massachusetts Avenue. In the Twenties and Thirties—Drew Pearson's days—an invitation to the British Embassy had, it seems, been regarded as offering some degree of social status. In my hearing a lady of Cabot-like pretensions suggested at the dinner table that when she was young, members of the House would have been glad to come to a British Embassy meal and do the washing up! The blunt facts on social clout were otherwise, and we in the Embassy knew that to be so. More to the taste of modern legislators was and, I believe, still is an invitation to a conference in the U.K.

(air passage paid) where they can "chew the fat" with a group of British Members of Parliament, legislative specialists and perhaps meet a minister or two of the Crown. Ditchley Park, a comfortable well-butlered early 18th century mansion a few miles north of Oxford, has been the site of a remarkably useful series of such meetings both during and after the Second World War.

Other diplomatic missions which took events on Capitol Hill very seriously were certainly the Japanese, the Canadians, the French and Germans and, somewhat later, the Russians. I had known the Soviet Charge d'Affaires Tchernikov in Geneva where he was my opposite number, so to speak. Over a Washington lunch about 1969 he asked me what I was doing, and I told him in general terms. Some two months later a young Soviet Embassy secretary called on Senator Everett McKinley Dirksen, colorful, given to histrionics, the Republican Minority Leader. One can only guess at what transpired but next day the rumbustious senator was on his feet in the Chamber castigating the effrontery of Soviet pipsqueaks. The later Soviet approach to the Hill was a good deal more sophisticated. The Japanese were always assiduous in their contacts, which came out in several Senate hearings into the activities of lobbyists. In the early Sixties the sugar quota had been the one commodity which seemed to provoke most jostling. A particularly presentable attaché from a Caribbean Mission was said to have complemented his activities on the Hill with those in a number of Georgetown beds.

"Cookie-pushing" in the nation's capital has been a diplomatic activity both expected and jeered at since Drew

Pearson's acidulous comments. Much business of course is done under these circumstances at lunches and dinners either in diplomatic surroundings—cocktails at our Massachusetts Avenue Rotunda, for example—or in clubs and restaurants. Bean soup lunches in the Capitol were an agreeable way of meeting members, far better than the distinctly indifferent restaurants in that area. There was certainly a good deal of home entertainment expected, both received and offered, quite apart from the innumerable national days and our own annual Queen's Birthday garden party in June with its highly traditional strawberries and cream. For the discharge of such courtesies one is much dependent on a good wife, one who does the careful and imaginative housekeeping required for entertainment on a limited budget. And it behooves her to be skillful and patient with servants, upon whom it is often hard to depend. Necessary also a good memory for names and faces. Constance possessed these qualities in generous measure and established warm relations with a number of wives of members of the Congress and the other diplomatic missions. She found rewarding chairing one of their discussion groups to one of which Barbara Bush often came.

Apart from being "our man on Capitol Hill," there were specific tasks in the Chancery to be done, and I enjoyed them: dispatch writing was one. The ambassador wanted drafts on topics of special interest to Her Majesty's Government which obviously included the progress of Kennedy-era innovations such as the Peace Corps, the march of Civil Rights, welfare experiments and so on. On these assignments I was lucky to have the shrewd help of a gifted lady First Secretary who later took a key job in our European Economic Community Mission in Brussels. She did much of the reporting on the weird and baffling convolutions of Watergate which became very much of a Special Subject. Some reporting dealt with procedural matters which might be helpful to the Clerk's Office in Westminster. At the time there was a rapidly increasing awareness of the value to the Parliament of Select Committees, a number of which were in fact established, though predictably the Whips had strong reservations - not being enchanted with the prospect of bipartisan viewpoints emerging from such new-fangled committees' hearings. The Legislative Reference section of the Library of Congress was very helpful with expert advice, and one remembers with gratitude the advice given so generously by former Congressman Gilbert Gude of Maryland who was then its head, as well as the assistance of the superb staff in the Office of the Speaker.

A diplomatic mission in any capital is first and foremost concerned with maintaining close touch with the foreign ministry of the country to which it is accredited. In Washington, despite the tendency of presidents and their White House advisers to side-step the State Department, it was at 2201 C Street that our country desk officers so-called spent much of their time. It was to be expected that they would substantially base their appreciations of how the Congress would vote on any issue from the assessments they were offered by the State Department which, in turn, relied on its own headcounters—as a rule very good at their job. But often I could be of help with ideas I had picked up on the Hill.

There is always plenty of information about in Washington on who is saying what and where everybody comes from. Apart from the daily press and the generous television and radio coverage of events, a student of Capitol Hill is well-served by the *Congressional Quarterly*, which seemed to me to have a Democratic tinge, and the *National Journal* which appeared to lean to the other side. There are dangers in Embassy staff consorting too closely with newspaper correspondents from their own land: only too easy for journalists to "coalesce" into one opinion, as Marvin Kalb is reported by Dr. Fenno to have admitted. Though I was on warm terms with our *Times* correspondent Louis Heren, later the general editor in London, I kept at some distance from our newspaper and radio correspondents, though being of course ready to offer them an introduction to a member or staff assistant, if asked.

Her Majesty's ambassadors—and I worked under no less than four during a long tour of duty— thought it sensible and right that their staff travelled widely through the U.S.A. They were most agreeable to me, accepting suggestions which members made that I should pay a visit to their states or districts, giving a talk or so here, meeting people and even joining their election campaign tours. There were obvious perils: one had to be careful that an electioneering type visit with a Republican was followed by one organised under the sign of the Democratic donkey. Excluding travel during my term at Harvard, I had a chance to visit all the States of the Union with the exception of Hawaii and Alaska. Not all such visits were without incident. Representative Bryan Dorn cordially invited me down to his fine old residence at Greenwood, South

Carolina. I cannot remember the precise importance of the occasion, but tables were spread on a field nearby, laden with beverages and favorite foods, which were rapidly consumed by his grateful Democratic constituents. Mr. Dorn, who had been the wonder-boy of S.C. politics, was indubitably a man who respected his country's Special Relationship with Britain, such as it then was. A handsome squad of Girl Grenadiers in shining silver and magenta uniforms treated us to fine renderings of "Tipperary," "Colonel Bogey" and, of course, the "British Grenadiers," my old regimental tune. In the evening, we sallied forth to the County Fair, where, amid a variety of diversions, there was a small enclosure equipped with a publicity tent and, to emphasise the point, a Democratic burro. About midnight, we decided to return to Greenwood and got into his sizeable car to quit the car park. But a very large vehicle blocked the way and would not move. Inside it we descried a female who was clearly very drunk. Our driver attempted to push past her but, in so doing, had the misfortune to graze the side of her car. Angry imprecations and fruity threats ensued and, as we left the fairground, we became aware that she was following us. We hoped to elude her by driving faster but to no avail. Twisting and turning up side roads equally failed to shake her off, for by that time we had become convinced that her intentions were not at all kindly and the Congressman certainly did not want to be involved in any reportable incident. Finally, after something like a twenty mile chase, we saw a police post at the side of the road. We roared up to it, the brakes were jammed on and my innocent friend leaped out and disappeared into the scrub. His administrative assistant then rushed into the station telling the astonished sergeant that there was a mean drunken driver close behind and, in the minor confusion, we were able to drive off and pick up Bryan Dorn further down the road. We were very glad the woman had not used a gun on us.

Looking back, a number of other trips are particularly vivid, among them an invitation to meet people in the mountain district by Jackson, Tennessee. There it was possible to talk with an old lady who talked Elizabethan English. That evening, I was entertained by the judge who produced from under his desk a bottle of fiery contraband with which to wash down the catfish and hush-puppies. The consequent hangover was dreadful! A visit to the innovative mayor of New Orleans together with my sister included a memorable lunch with the egregious Leander Perez in his quarters on that hurricane-lashed strip of land out in the gulf, Plaquemines Parish. The then Governor of Louisiana received us, I remember, with both feet on his desk; that was, however, before he went to jail. A much more fruitful and more considerable interview was that with Governor Jimmy Carter, who told me quite early on that he had in mind to run for the White House in 1976. Seeing the deserted shoe factories of Maine brought home to me what Senator Bill Hathaway had often emphasized, that there would be great pressure to seek to impose quotas on foreign footwear. (In all conscience, we had our own out-of-date industrial sites at home.)

Attending national political conventions was also an interesting course on the menu. In Chicago, I missed getting mixed up in the 1968 hurly-burly in Grant Park though several M.P.'s did not: the young grandson of

A Capitol Fellow

Churchill was at one point grabbed by a burly cop and asked for his name. "So, you're Winston Churchill," he growled. "Well, my name is Thomas Jefferson!" Waiting in our Chicago consul's house, we received a telephone call from the police. "We have a dame here who says she is a Member of Parliament. But we think she is drunk!" She certainly was a Member, but C.S. gas, one felt, was a more likely reason for her dizziness in the paddy-wagon.

Coming down to join me at the 1972 Republican Convention, my sister was taken in charge, despite her ticket, for having in her purse a small sandwich knife, which she had made use of in Vermont a few days earlier. Since she hardly looked militant, a promise was eventually made of return. Security was indeed tight, and the palm-trees outside the convention hall resounded with the thumps of nightsticks being exercised on their trunks. Chicago Republican Ed Derwinski, whom I had asked for a ticket just in case I did not get one from the regular State Department liaison section, regretted that he only had one with the inscription, "Ukrainians for Nixon." I took it along. Entering the convention hall, it was plain that the diplomatic reserved enclosure was full. The Japanese ambassador and his wife were standing disconsolately, their seats disgracefully appropriated by a brash crowd of young persons sporting Nixon badges. Asked why they were there, these youngsters artlessly confirmed what had been roundly denied by G.O.P. headquarters —that their trip to Miami had been wholly financed by the party. So for that couple of days at any rate, I became an American Ukrainian.

A melancholy experience was the New Orleans funeral of Hale Boggs, the House Majority Leader presumed dead in an Alaskan air crash. In Jackson Square, we stood as guns boomed out a final salute. Quite close was ex-President Lyndon B. Johnson, frail, his hair blued, looking ill. He seemed to be shaken by each cannonblast. I had a word with him at the subsequent reception and was very likely the last Englishman to have done so. He was dead within a very few days.

Tremendous changes in attitudes to ethnic questions over those years are now clearly recognisable. When I first travelled down to Arkansas and Alabama, the bull-whip of Sheriff Connor was not far away. Mark, now Lord Bonham Carter and I, were given in personal detail by Mr. John Doar, then Assistant Attorney General, a grim account of how much harassment of blacks was still going on. Mr. Hodding Carter, down from New York as new editor of the leading paper in Greenville, Mississippi, was sitting on the steps of his house night after night with a shotgun on his knees. By the time President Nixon was in his second term, the situation had changed strikingly, and what is more important, irreversibly. Also the Melting Pot had grained out in a way which would have astonished observers twenty years before. People no longer wished to render themselves all of one received American configuration. Italians were now ready to be recognised as American-Italians. Jewish organisations and individuals were proud to stand clearly out and exercise their special cultural, political and economic flair. Spanish-speaking immigrants, legal or otherwise, were beginning to impose a certain recognition by virtue of their numbers. Even

Polish Americans, hitherto something of a butt for jokes, were now insistent on their individual identity. And significantly, by the Seventies, persons of Anglo stock were a minority of the total population of the United States. Ten years of enormous changes, with immigration—legal and illegal—continuing at a strong pace.

These were some of the changes witnessed over a decade in which the Congress played an essential role in the great triarchy of President, Congress and Judiciary. Looking back now, some twenty years later, it seems that a foreign diplomat assigned to specialise in congressional relations must first of all read as much as he or she can absorb about what is going on. And that is made a good deal easier by the daily production of the *Congressional Record*, an astonishing, unique document in that it contains "extensions of remarks" - in fact speeches which might have been made on the floor but which, sometimes mercifully, never came across the sound system. Professional analyses of the state of individual pieces of legislation are usually available. Voting records over years are published, so it is pretty simple to gauge the likely attitude of a member on most issues, barring arm-twisting by the whips. But absolutely indispensable is a steady determination to maintain integrity and keep confidences. Failure on Capitol Hill (or off it) to respect a tip-off or the privacy of a criticism means an immediate and usually terminal loss of credibility. Nor will any attempt to play one member off against another do other than fail disastrously.

CHAPTER TWELVE

HOME TO ROOST

The offer of a short fellowship at Harvard came as a completely unexpected and very pleasant surprise. The proposal was that Constance and I should go up to Harvard in January, 1974 to the Institute of Politics at the Kennedy School of Government and use it as a base for talks, discussions and a bit of travel until late in May, when we should be on our way home to the U.K. We said our goodbyes accordingly in Washington and, toward the end of that month, took the train up to Cambridge and on to Winthrop House, where the Master had very courteously offered us the John F. Kennedy suite. The Foreign Office, whom I had already told that I wished to retire, believing that I was getting stale, decided to look on the period at Harvard as a sabbatical. At Harvard it was settled that I should give a course which, though offering no credits to students, would discuss the American Congress against a background of European political assemblies, in particular the Westminster Parliament. So far as the Embassy desk was concerned, Pauline, my assistant, would and did cope admirably until a successor arrived.

As things turned out several friends from both Houses of Congress were good enough to come up to Cambridge, address the group and stimulate our discussions. One surmised that, once away from the Hill, far from constituents and needling correspondents, politicians might feel a good deal freer to bounce ideas about. Of course Boston being so near, we at the School witnessed some of the motions of the Kennedy political machine, and several of my fellow Fellows were in some way so connected. Not so my roommate Alan Otten of the *Wall Street Journal*, whose writing I had always admired as terse and sagacious. People were extremely nice to us and gave us the chance to meet a variety of distinguished and delightful scholars whose acquaintance we should otherwise never have made. As a rule, we took our meals with the students in the refectory and enjoyed the excellent fare provided in Winthrop House. We thus met Pierre Fortin, the house tutor, who greatly helped us to fit in, at our rather advanced age, with the students close to whom we lived. Pierre, a remarkable summa cum laude lawyer, afterwards worked in London and is now running his own firm of international attorneys from a historic palazzo in Rome.

Apart from its superb libraries, Harvard is a very pleasant university to wander about in. We liked the green, tree-lined surroundings despite cold Spring weather, and the river close by, with racing shells moving determinedly along. Boston was also so handy and had plenty to offer, including the state legislature. We were shown a great deal by an old friend, Joe Harsch of the *Christian Science*

Monitor, whom I had known in London years before. His Boston Club seemed extremely reminiscent of traditional clubs at home— fubsy and relaxed. But there is a big difference between that decorum and the more earthy truculence of South Boston. I admit to have been a little shaken to watch Senator Edward Kennedy striding down its main street on St. Patrick's day with a posse of companions armed with shillelaghs. I retired to the nearest pub but found the talk there, which was not unassisted by copious libations of black beer and whiskey, so extremely disobliging in respect of Queen and Constitution that prudence suggested anonymity and a tactful withdrawal to Cambridge.

In May, we flew West to San Francisco where we stayed in Berkeley with Nelson and Linda Polsby. I had originally met Nelson at a seminar in Washington where we discussed legislative reforms. He then struck me as just the right sort of specialist participant for the annual American Legislators Conference at Ditchley Park, which I mentioned in the last chapter. I went along with him to that meeting early in 1974 and we both enjoyed it. About three years later, Nelson took a sizeable sabbatical in the United Kingdom armed with a few introductions to Members of Parliament and their staff. Very soon his acquaintance in Westminster and outside it had increased mightily. Certainly he got to know most of the political scientists in Britain, too often working in underfunded institutes, a situation which has sadly shown little improvement, most recently due to the economic slump. Then Nelson and his family went back to Berkeley, returned East to teach awhile at Harvard at the Kennedy

School, and finally established in Berkeley his lively and imaginative Institute of Governmental Studies to which he lures foreign political affairs scholars to their collegial pleasure and to the benefit of his students on campus.

More closely, and with a great deal more personal insight than most American political scientists, Polsby follows the deep changes today going on in the British Parliamentary system. Two out of the three major political parties, for instance, are talking seriously about electoral reform. Largely inspired by a series of studies of the Congress and its procedures, Westminster has seen since the late Sixties the formation of a series of select committees in the House of Commons. Unwelcome to the party whips, who tend to see a challenge to their authority in the emergence from committee discussions of an all-party view, there is every likelihood that these select committees, covering an ever larger spectrum of administration, will grow and become more influential. I had been able, in a very minor way, to become involved in the various exchanges between the Speaker's Office, the Library of Congress and the Clerk of the House of Commons and his enlarged staff, and much enjoyed this facet of my work. There is little doubt that several recent reforms and innovations in Westminster derive directly from that dialogue, among them the substantial improvement in the salaries of Members of Parliament and the provision to them of a modicum of paid staff assistance, which fifty years ago, at any rate, had been minimal—a small cupboard allotted grudgingly to each Member, together with a few sheets of notepaper each day!

Part way through our stay at the Polsby eyrie on the slopes of Grizzly Peak, Constance and I were able to increase our previous slight knowledge of California, this time touring north of San Francisco with the superb coastal views and the impressive breakers of the Pacific. We were careful not totally to omit the Napa Valley vineyards. Then back to Cambridge, goodbyes and return to Europe on an Italian liner, the "Leonardo da Vinci." It was a sad voyage in a way. We were leaving many friends made over a decade. The ship was very shortly to be taken out of service as uneconomic. The crew were sullen and rude to those elderly Italians who had made their money in the land of opportunity and were now returning to display their wealth to their kin and then die. Voyages on ships appeal to us both: the routine of living aboard, the elaborately ordered meals and a half-conscious sense of historical adventure on the high seas are all so much to set against the huddled squalor of a long distance airflight.

Soon we were looking at Lisbon, where a revolution — by good fortune peaceful— had taken place with the substitution of a democratic government for the old Salazar dictatorship. Then on to Genoa, disembarcation, train and familiar Dover with its unimpressive line of Edwardian hotels under the chalk cliffs. We had no house to reoccupy. Constance had insisted on selling our suburban cottage at the top of the market the year before, so we were not unequipped to think of buying another. Nevertheless, we lacked enthusiasm for a new Foreign Office posting, either at home or abroad—especially London, where the conditions of life had worsened so noticeably during the fifteen years we had been away. I was

Home To Roost

a few months short of the statutory sixty year mark. Some different job perhaps, such as that of secretary to the Lord Mayor of London, might be attractive, provided we could find somewhere to live we liked. It was piquant to be escorted for an interview, almost conspiratorially, up the back stairs of the old Guildhall by a flunkey in 18th century costume. A retired admiral piped me to the post. So off we went to visit friends in the West Country and determined to have a look round at houses, just in case one of them met our imaginings on the subject of decorous country life.

We had seen and rejected a number of overpriced dwellings in Cornwall and Dorset and had moved over to Somerset. In the old town of Sherborne we called in, rather perfunctorily, at a realtor, and were told that a house was on the market a few miles away in West Coker. We went to see it and were both immediately captured. It was what we had thought of as ideal—old, rambling, well-kept and had a fine, well-stocked garden. The owner, a retired general and his wife wanted a larger place for their children and grandchildren. The deal was struck and we soon moved in. What we did not know was the quite extraordinary fact that West Coker, a village referred to by George Hardy under the pseudonym Narrabourne, had, some four hundred years earlier, been where Drowers lived and worked.

The history of Marlborough Cottage is clearly recorded. It was originally built as a double cottage— probably to hold a dozen souls—just after the English Revolution of 1685. King James II had fled to France; there was a shrewd Dutch prince on the English throne. Flax was produced hereabouts to be made into canvas and ropes. The walls are one foot thick, of hamstone, a golden-tinged limestone from a hilltop quarry opened by the Romans who built villas in the area. For the time being at least we are protected by environmental legislation against development opposite and can look up the field sweeping up to the 400 foot Coker Ridge with its ancient carter's track.

A newcomer still requires a number of years to find real acceptance in most British villages, and little West Coker is no exception. But after about five Christmases had passed including an attempt at a village history, I was very ready to do something more than minor decorations, resiting of flower-beds and visits to the surrounding sights. British civil service tradition, despite the introduction of various forms of political commissar by recent Tory regimes, is strongly against political identification with any party or group. So we had both concealed over the years our party-political tendencies! (Constance is herself by nature a conservative.) For years my own growing political sympathies were, so far as Britain was concerned, with our third party—the Liberals—who had never recovered from the opportunistic hands of David Lloyd George after the 1914-1918 war.

So in 1980, at the suggestion of a local friend Paddy Ashdown, I was running for our local seat on the 57 strong Somerset County Council, a body elected for four year terms, representing some half million people. Ashdown himself, with a predominately military background, was courting the Yeovil Parliamentary constituency and eyeing the seat of the Tory incumbent, about to retire. Yeovil—three miles from our village—used to be purely a Liberal market town, which also traditionally produced gloves and ropes. Early this century its commercial character changed. Industrial workers from the bleak North and the Midlands came down to take jobs in its large helicopter production plant which was of importance in two world wars. The Labour Party has never done well in the Yeovil area—or indeed in the West of England as a whole. So Ashdown might count on a strong vote going beyond Liberal support at the polling booth.

The next Spring fortune smiled and for the following eight years I represented some twelve thousand people including eleven villages. The 1985 local elections in Somerset gave the Liberals for the first time a majority over the Tories, and I found myself in the County Council chair. Up to that time serried ranks of landowners and retired military had regularly assumed that they had some God-given right to local rule! Education, the police, libraries, highways and the environment are the main preoccupations of county councils, housing being currently divided between central government and the small district councils.

The Conservatives scraped back at the height of the short-lived Thatcher boom but the last Somerset county elections put the Liberal Democrats firmly back in power. As I write, the government in Westminster is seeking to reduce the power of county councils, one reason naturally being that it cannot still count on the support of the "shires," such as Somerset.

Paddy Ashdown is so far little known in the United States, not surprisingly since the Liberal Democrats, unassisted by proportional representation, dispose only a few seats in the House of Commons. But he may well have an increasingly important national role as he gains political experience and learns how to take, and how to reject advice. His temporary alliance with David Owen (Lord Owen — the recent colleague of Cyrus Vance) had caused the change of party name from Liberals to Liberal Democrats. To be sure Owen was no easy bedfellow.

Local politics within and without the confines of the United States have much in common. So here in Somerset, after a decade the other side of the Atlantic, I had at once felt a familiarity with more than one of the issues which came before my desk. The more pleasant it was therefore, when I stood down after eight years on our council, to receive a Californian invitation from the I.G.S. to return to Berkeley as a visiting scholar and spend some weeks on campus. Here was an excellent opportunity to hobnob, not only with American students and academics but also with relaxed representatives of political faculties in Germany, Sweden, Italy, Bulgaria and Japan, all of whom were good company. And now Nelson Polsby has succeeded in persuading the cash-strapped Foreign Office to join with him in a new initiative promising more exchanges, scholarly and practical, with a variety of ideas which can only help counteract tempting isolationist prejudices, political as well as commercial, on both sides of the Atlantic, not to mention the burgeoning Pacific sphere. These misunderstandings, many artificially stimulated, are just as likely to fester in Europe as in the U.S.A., and we should all be on our guard.

POSTSCRIPT

"The horror of that moment," the King went on, "I shall never, NEVER forget!" "You will, though," the Queen said, "If you don't make a memorandum of it."

Lewis Carroll

On the desk the other day was a list of the small boys who were with me at school early in 1924. Over one quarter had lost their fathers in the first World War. Today very few of those boys are still alive. I do not, in all frankness, find this particularly depressing since I was never an "Old Boy" type, but it does produce a kind of gratitude which should be offered to the Fates, at least that one has been lucky enough to slip away cat-like from more than one disaster. And are there not so many occupations in which people linger without hope of escape, awful jobs with dreadful bosses or forced companions?

Too much about long-past prisoner of war recollections are probably related here. I am very well aware that the vast sufferings of millions of people in Europe and the Soviet Union, especially the carefully graduated horrors of the Holocaust, make these personal experiences simply insignificant. One lesson my grandfather taught us children was that rancour is close to bigotry and thoroughly nasty. Possibly I have been fortunate since 1945 in being able to make friends with Japanese, though some of my former comrades still find this impossible. When Constance and I first came to Washington, the very able First Secretary of the Japanese Embassy was a Mr. Kazuo Chiba. We occasionally met for lunch to discuss events, and Constance and I found him and his wife most pleasant and agreeable people. How nice to know that he quite recently served as Ambassador for Japan at the Court of St. James's!

On the lawn below, magpies, who do not sing, are chasing away the thrushes.